A
HELLUVA
HIGH NOTE

A HELLUVA HIGH NOTE

Surviving Life, Love, and *American Idol*

Kara DioGuardi

itbooks

AN IMPRINT OF HARPERCOLLINS PUBLISHERS

HarperCollins books may be purchased for educational, business, or sales promotional use.
For information please write: Special Markets Department, HarperCollins Publishers,
10 East 53rd Street, New York, NY 10022.

FIRST EDITION

Designed by Jennifer Daddio / Bookmark Design & Media Inc.

Library of Congress Cataloging-in-Publication Data
DioGuardi, Kara.
   A helluva high note : surviving life, love, and American Idol / Kara DioGuardi. — 1st ed.
      p.   cm.
   Includes index.
   ISBN 978-0-06-205989-5
   1. DioGuardi, Kara.   2. Singers—United States—Biography.   3. American Idol (Television
program) I. Title.
   ML420.D563A3 2011
   782.42164092—dc22
   [B]   2010048938

11 12 13 14 15 OV/RRD 10 9 8 7 6 5 4 3 2 1

This book is dedicated to you—the reader

May you find your passion in life and make it your purpose.

May you find the resolve to face your deepest fears and

overcome them, and lastly may you have the courage

to follow your dreams so that you will never know regret.

On a lighter note, when reading this memoir, I hope

you laugh at times and are able to find humor

in your own dark moments, too. Without that

I would have been truly lost.

—KARA DIOGUARDI

Contents

Preface

think of this book as the longest song I've ever written. In a way it's the soundtrack to my life. It takes you through the events that inspired my music and influenced me to be the person I am today. My way of storytelling is truer to the art of songwriting than it is to penning memoirs because that's what I know and do best. When you sit with the page—or with your collaborators, in the case of songwriting—you never really know what piece of your past, present, or future is going to surface. But it's good to leave yourself open to the surprise. What will you tap into this time? An unresolved feeling about a parent? A letter you wish you had sent to a lost love but didn't? Or a fear you thought was long dormant until it reawoke with a vengeance? You pull from different memories even though why you may be reflecting again on a moment from five years ago isn't quite clear. When you listen to your inner voice, it has an uncanny way of telling you what you have and haven't dealt with yet and what you need to look at in order to move forward.

Each chapter of this book recounts a memory, experience, or, in some cases, an issue I've really struggled with and conquered. Not surprisingly, these major life themes found their way into my music—sometimes many years later, when I finally came to understand their influence on me and the fact that so many others had felt these feelings at some point, too. I named the chapters after these songs so you would ultimately know the events in my life that helped give rise to them. I also included anecdotes that reveal a little bit about that day in the studio, in the car, in the gym, on iChat (where I wrote "This" with Darius Rucker and Frank Rogers), or wherever else my cowriters and I were physically, mentally, and emotionally on the day a particular song was born. Hopefully you will get a sense of how real-life experiences on the part of me and those I've written with translate into music.

If you're not a songwriter, you may be asking "What's in this book for me?" And that's a good question because at first it may seem a little like that "forgotten event from five years ago"—the one that wasn't all that relevant until it was keeping you up at night again. The truth is, if you are, or have ever been, in search of yourself, needing inspiration, or looking for love in all the wrong places, even if just for a nanosecond on the big clock of life, then we have shared something in common and this book is for you. I have spent most of my years trying to figure out who I am and why I do what I do, whether I'm asking myself this for the sake of my art or for my own well-being (usually it's for the latter). Through the answers I've uncovered, I've been able to heal myself and help others who are asking the same questions.

Too many of us are born into families and communities that have built-in belief systems we are expected to blindly follow. Frankly, I grew up feeling trapped by traditions and expectations that had nothing to do with who I am or what I wanted to be. But thank God for my inner rebel. I spent lots of time probing my needs and desires and developing my voice—both my sing-ing voice and my writing voice. In retrospect, I credit my darkest times—and there have been many—with making it impossible for me *not* to face my demons. Fortunately, the light on the other side of that introspection made up for all the pain.

It's never easy to evaluate yourself or the direction of your life, but I highly recommend it. You never know when you're going to need to draw from the clarity and strength it provides. And you don't want to go on piling up "could haves" and "should haves" in life either.

I owe a lot of gratitude to the writers and artists I've worked with along the way who made me feel safe enough to share my deepest secrets. They helped me face the corners of my soul that I never would have even peered into without them. They listened, comforted, and reminded me that I wasn't alone.

If you walk away after reading this book even slightly more in tune with your own needs, desires, and fears, or feeling the least bit inspired to find your true voice, then I've succeeded in my goal. That is what this book is all about—finding the courage to reach for your own personal high notes in life even if it means falling flat more often than not. Most of what I have learned in life has been through my failures, not my successes. I've experienced both and some in very public forums, but I'm all the better for it, as you'll soon find out.

—Kara DioGuardi
Prospect, Maine, July 2010

P.S.—In a couple of places, I've changed, or left out entirely, the names of individuals who have played a role in my life in order to protect their privacy. In a few places, I've altered details, locales, and other specifics to be sure these people are not recognizable, but in no instance have I altered or changed the stories that I am sharing with you.

Acknowledgments

'd like to thank and give a round of applause to . . . Hope Innelli, for not hanging up on me when I said I wanted to write the book. You were my partner, sounding board, psychiatrist, and champion. You helped me tell my story and there would be no *Helluva High Note* without your extensive contributions. I am forever indebted to you for the blood, sweat, and tears you put into this book. You're an unsung hero of the publishing world, but I will always be singing your praises. All the people at HarperCollins . . . Michael Morrison, Carrie Kania, Kim Lewis, Beth Silfin, Andrea Molitor, Lisa Thong, Heidi Metcalfe, Kevin Callahan, Michael Barrs, Susan Amster.

Simon Green, Jonathan Swaden, and Jeff Frasco at CAA.

Danica Smith, for her PR genius.

Clyde Lieberman, for the hours you spent on the phone encouraging me. If I didn't emphasize it enough in the book, please know it did not go unnoticed. Brook Morrow and Larry Flick, for their constant belief and friendship. Jaime Roberts, for his continued moral support and legal guidance through the years. Stephen Finfer, for being an extraordinary partner and for the photos I always complained about you taking, one of which is on the cover of the book. And John Rudolph and Bug Music for watching over my life's work.

Joe DioGuardi for teaching me the value of hard work and never giving up.

John DioGuardi for being the best brother anyone could ask for.

Suzie Paxton for being the sister I never had.

Michael McCuddy for showing me that when you meet the right person all the best love songs ever written come to life. The rest of my family, both biological and extended . . . you know who you are.

And lastly, *American Idol* for including me in a piece of its extraordinary history.

Introduction:

THE FOURTH JUDGE

The Fourth Judge.

When you say it out loud it sounds completely harmless. Like a Fourth Street, a fourth date, the fourth time. Little did I know that three simple words (yes, I counted right this time) would shake up my behind-the-scenes life in such a remarkable, exhilarating, but mostly gut-wrenching way.

It was first relayed to me that *American Idol* was looking for a fourth judge when I was in my agent's office (how ridiculously Hollywood does that sound?) and he closed the door to say, "I've put you on a short list to be the fourth judge on *American*

Idol." I looked at him, completely confused, then smiled as if he had told a good joke. Was he serious?

"What are you talking about? Why do they need a fourth judge?" I asked.

America, understandably, would soon be asking the same question. Why fix something that wasn't broken? The show's ratings were phenomenal and everyone loved the judges. I should have known right then that there would be problems. Looking back, I was naive to think that the proposition of *Idol*, with all its cachet and promise of celebrity, wasn't more like having a fully loaded gun propped in my mouth and ready to go off at any time.

I left the office not even considering the possibility that I'd ever be asked to join the famous judging panel. I was incredibly nonchalant about it all because, truth be told, I had probably only watched one full episode before that day. I was immersed in my career as a songwriter, A&R executive at Warner Bros., producer and co-owner of Arthouse Entertainment, a music publishing company. I never had time for television other than episodes of *Law & Order* (I am obsessed with Sam Waterston and love to watch him take those creeps down). Plus, I'd worked with a lot of the idols after their victories, and I didn't want to be overly influenced by the singers' performances on the show. I wanted to keep an open mind about their musical styles and abilities for when I met them in person.

A few weeks later I got a call to meet the producers of the show and several of the network executives. Could they be serious about this whole fourth judge thing? Despite these nagging questions, I put on my best tight skirt and bought a designer blouse (because, let's be honest, the sweatpants and vintage tee that I usually wore to the studio weren't going to cut it) and I walked confidently into the meeting at 19 Entertainment.

I entered with a cool, empowered demeanor because I never thought for one second that the interview would amount to anything. The one familiar face I saw was Simon Fuller's. He is the powerhouse behind *Idol*, the owner of 19 Entertainment, which looks after many of the contestants, including some who have earned the *Idol* title, and he is the manager for other celebrity talents including the Eurythmics, Spice Girls, and Victoria and David Beckham, just to name a few. Talk about an entertainment mogul. Since I had briefly been in the band Platinum Weird with Fuller's client Dave Stewart, he had to have known about the duo's failure, and maybe even about my brief stint on *The One*, an ABC summer music show in 2007 that garnered the lowest debut ratings that season and was yanked off the air in its second week. Yikes, seeing Fuller started to bring back the memory of these unfortunate back-to-back failures! As if that wasn't bad enough, all these other self-sabotaging thoughts crept into my head, like, *Why hadn't he told the others? Surely they wouldn't have taken the meeting.* I became painfully self-conscious. I didn't look anything like a star. But as I now know, nobody does until the stylists put a million pounds of makeup on you and tease your hair to high heaven. As you can imagine, it was an intense meeting. Nobody really spoke too much, which made me talk even more (a nasty little habit that reared its ugly head whenever I was nervous and would later make Simon Cowell want to duct-tape my mouth shut).

Then we got to the subject of the past season. Crap, I never watched it. Who was Carly Smithson, Michael Johns, and that guy with the dreads? *Help!* I thought. *Do I bullshit my way through this interview or be honest with them?* I chose honesty and I think they liked that I had the balls to admit I had never watched a full season of the biggest show in American television history.

I walked out of the meeting feeling flattered that they had even thought of me, and believing that the chances were slim to none that I would get the gig. I was also sworn to secrecy and told that if I so much as mentioned the meeting or the fact that they were looking for another judge to ANYONE, I would be out of the running. In addition, I imagined I'd never get to work with another *Idol* contestant again. Lucky for them, I was good at keeping secrets.

I must have done something right during that initial interview because a few weeks later I was en route to London to speak with Simon Cowell. Entering the BMG music building that day felt like being twenty-one all over again and playing my demo tape for someone who could potentially give me my first record deal. He could put me on the biggest show in America, which in my mind was like winning the lottery, or he could throw me back into my life as a songwriter, which at the time was starting to feel like sex in the missionary position. I was weary from the long flight but had arrived prepared. I studied the entire prior season and had come to understand why America loved to hate Simon so much while secretly wanting to be just like him. I felt that way, too, especially after watching countless hours of *American Idol*'s past auditions on YouTube. He was one of those bad boys you dated in college who had a wicked sense of humor and looked great on paper. You know, one of those guys you thought would eventually change his naughty ways. But that wasn't very likely in this case, considering that those ways made Simon $50 million a year. Man boobs or not, this guy was a serious star.

"Hello, *Kahra*," he said, puffing on a Newport menthol. The moment I entered his London office in the BMG building is when the correct pronunciation of my name went out the window. I don't even think he knew my last name. Thank God; can you imagine what he would have done with that? In his defense, I have never met a Brit who didn't call me "Kahra." They never get that first *a* right.

"Darling, sit down." This guy was good—and he smoked, which gave me my first line. "Can I bum a cigarette?" I asked. " Of course you can," he replied. Hmm, he made me want to smoke. Not a good sign. What was even worse was that the cigarettes were menthol and I immediately got a head rush.

The conversation started with us wondering how we had never met and him telling me how much he loved the song "Spinning Around," which I had cowritten with Paula Abdul. In fact, it was used on *Pop Idol*, the British precursor to *American Idol*. Apparently, when the producers saw Paula's name on the credits, they thought of her for *Idol*. *Wow, could our song have had something to do with her getting the gig?* I thought, still dizzy from the minty tobacco.

Simon really didn't know much about me, but then again I didn't really care. I was there to dazzle him, impress him with my newly acquired knowledge of the show after all my studying, beg him for the role that, by now, I was convinced was a once-in-a-lifetime opportunity. It's funny how getting closer to landing this job made me so hungry for it that I could almost taste it. I tried to make myself look like a star that day, spending a good twenty minutes on my face instead of applying the usual two strokes of mascara at the first red light while driving and one stroke of lipstick at the next. I remember having a big zit and wanting to angle myself so that he wouldn't see it. I swear I saw his eye brush over it quickly. I think he called me cute at one point, which, by the way, I didn't take as a compliment. What was I, a puppy?

"Well, Kahra, I'm glad we met . . . blah blah blah, and I'll see you in August." Wait, what? That's it? No interview. All he said was, "You have good energy and I think you'll be great for the show." You've got to be shitting me. I traveled six hours the day before my best friend's wedding weekend and that's it! @@#$##.

But . . . I got the gig. I wanted to scream and shout, and text just about everyone I knew, right then and there. Of course, I played it cool instead. Simon told me that if I needed any advice or help to call him and then he gave me his number.

And just like that, at approximately 4:40 London time on June 25, 2008, I became "Kahra, the polarizing fourth judge on *American Idol.*"

Or did I? I was floating on air when, several weeks later, I got a confusing call from my agent, who said that I needed to take a screen test, as a formality.

"What is that? You mean like an actress-type screen test?" I asked.

"It's just so the network can see you on TV. It's nothing," he assured me.

To my surprise, this "no-big-deal screen test" consisted of me watching prior contestants on a small TV monitor and commenting on their performances once the producers paused the tape for me to speak. I can only imagine what I looked like straining to hear and see them on the tiny screen. When this makeshift video was sent to the network, they got nervous. They decided to reroute some of the contestants from San Francisco to Los Angeles for the preliminary auditions (the ones prior to the auditions America sees on television). This gave me a chance to judge contestants in person alongside two of the producers. That's when I first met Adam Lambert. He had a great voice, but was doing this very dramatic thing with his eyes. The producers weren't sure about him, speculating that Cowell might not like him, but I said, " No way. We've got to put him through," and thank God we did. Can you imagine a Season 8 without his rendition of Johnny Cash's "Ring of Fire," Tears for Fears' "Mad World," or Nina Simone's "Feeling Good"?

Of course, I passed this screen test with flying colors. I was funny (something I never really was again on *Idol*), comfortable, and totally myself. I was in like Flynn. When I left the auditions that day, I could visualize myself being on the panel. I began to feel seduced by the promise of celebrity. What's more, I was ready for it. I was older and I had knowledge that would keep me away from the obvious pitfalls of fame—there would be no tapes of drunken nights out, no photos snatched of me without underwear, no evidence of me cheating. These things would never happen. I was a soon-to-be-happily-married, thirtysomething, successful music professional who had passed her screen test and who really wanted to help young talent get their big break. So what could be the downside?

Two years, one month, and nine days later, I would wake up on the coast of Maine, where I was vacationing, to news that I was FIRED. I have only felt that sick to my stomach two times in my life. Once when my mother was undergoing a six-hour surgery to treat ovarian cancer and I was anxiously waiting outside the OR for the doctors to tell me if she would live or die; and then again when I broke up with my former boyfriend whom I thought I would marry someday. (That, of course, was before I met my husband, the man I was really destined to be with.)

Here it was again. That "Will I ever get through this? Am I going to collapse? Is this how it feels right before you die?" feeling. No one even gave me a heads-up that my job was in jeopardy. In fact, just two weeks before I was speaking to an executive producer about the upcoming season's schedule. Then again, who really ever knows that their bosses are considering replacing them? Lucky for me, the janitorial closet they called my dressing room had long been disassembled, so no walk down the corridors with my personal effects in hand was necessary. Instead I had to endure what felt like endless speculation in the media about my future. When the story first broke, I naturally thought I had been fired, but that rumor was negated when I spoke with the network executives and the producers by phone. Unfortunately, it was too late—I had already gone through the full range of emotions one goes through when they think they're losing their job. The sickest part about the whole thing is that I burst into tears at the very thought of being FIRED. I didn't cry because I loved the show, or was really into being a celebrity, or because I was disappointed over the prospect of losing millions of dollars. I cried because I was being rejected and disrespected publicly—but mostly because I was being rejected. It tapped into the hurt I felt all those years when I was in my early twenties pounding the pavement back in New York City and having doors shut in my face—that painful time before anyone ever cut a song of mine. It conjured up all the angst I had felt when my dad told me I could have done better on my SATs. And it stirred up all the insecurities I learned to squelch whenever my heart got broken by a boy. Rejection, in a nutshell, sucks, and I wondered after all these years how the hell I ended up there again.

One

SPINNING AROUND

"I'm spinning around,
move out of my way . . .
I'm breaking it down,
I'm not the same."

've always had a fascination with objects that spin around with incredible precision but still maintain a hint of chaos. Objects such as carousels or tops. I even enjoyed spinning myself. As a kid, I remember going to my ballet class with Mrs. Beavis. (I swear that was her real name!) She had a long, swanlike figure that made you immediately feel like you lacked any sort of grace, which, of course, we all did at eight years old. I hated the pliés, the grand jetés, the fifth position, but when it came to learning fouettés, where you spin around until you are on the verge of throwing up, I realized that I had found my move and I busted it out as often as I could. I loved the sensation of whirling around in a controlled state knowing full well that my ass could be laid out on the floor at any minute. I didn't have a clue that I was physically acting out what would be the first twenty years of my life. I would spin for a long time until I hit the bottom and had to stop, reevaluate, and pick myself up off the ground.

I was born on December 9, 1970, in White Plains, New York. I really did a job on my poor mother, who suffered from toxemia during her pregnancy and had to have an emergency C-section, as both of our lives were at stake. She said I came into this world with a vengeance and a mission. Although it would take me a minute to find my groove, she was right.

Music was the universal language in my family. I cannot remember a day when I didn't hear it. Whether it was my nanny Mary, my maternal grandmother playing Debussy's "Clair de Lune" on the piano, or my father's mother, Nanny Grace, singing "When the Red Red Robin" or my mother blasting Frankie Valli and the Four Seasons on the oldies station in her Ford Pinto. (I loved that car but could have done without her smoking with the windows rolled up. It was *so Mad Men*.)

My mother's family consisted of many aspiring opera singers and musicians. My great-grandfather had made quite a lot of money in the stonemasonry business, helping to build many of the oldest buildings in New York City. He rewarded his children with trips to Italy, where they would study music and voice. The star of the family was my great-aunt Theresa, who as a six-year-old was even praised by the Italian composer Respighi, at St. Cecelia's Conservatory of Music in Rome. Years later she would find herself playing alongside Charles Mingus. As the story goes, she liked a recording she had heard of Lennie Tristano, a famous blind pianist, so she wandered into his midtown studio and introduced herself. All these jazz heavyweights like Charlie Mingus, Stan Getz, Max Roach, and Bud Powell were there, stoned and laughing, as my prim and proper, red-lipstick-wearing, Jackie Kennedy–pillbox-hat-toting, walking dichotomy of an aunt asked to play a four-hand with Tristano! She let loose and tore it up that day, and became friends with all of them, including Mingus, with whom she eventually got the chance to play.

Most of my grandmother's brothers and sisters wanted to make a living from music. It was their passion. But only my aunt succeeded in that goal. There were even rumblings that one great-uncle fell gravely ill with depression because his dream of being an opera singer was never realized. These Pizzutellos (my nanny's maiden name) were sensitive, and rejection cut them deep at the core. Unfortunately, success in music, or any field for that matter, is about taking the chances, absorbing the blows, and staying in the fight. Come to think of it, maybe I've been channeling a bit of my aunt Teresa all these years.

By contrast, my father's family wasn't trying to break into the music business; they just LOVED music. They were especially attached to the Rat Packers—Frank Sinatra, Tony Bennett, and Dean Martin. My grandfather would pull up in his blue '65 Caddie smoking a cigar with the eight-track blasting Sinatra's "My Way." My grandmother loved to sing and dance to whatever was playing. She was four feet ten inches tall and always wore a five-inch heel. Talk about calf muscles. I learned every nursery rhyme I know from her.

As much as music was a part of my life growing up, I'd be lying if I told you that I knew I wanted to be a singer from the minute I could form a sentence.

While I loved singing and dancing, I also loved playing barkeeper downstairs in my parents' basement, where I used Monopoly money as currency and handwritten menus my dad copied for me at his office to list the daily fare. I would arrange folding tables into four or five stations just like in a restaurant and I'd play all the roles, from waitress, bartender, owner—and my personal favorite, money changer. I would even bust out a song now and then so my joint was a bit different from everyone else's. Truth is, I was a "hyphenate" even back then—a creative and businessperson all in one. I knew it at an early age, so why the hell did I let others convince me differently? Ah, hindsight is always 20/20—I wish I'd bought shares in that little company named after a fruit a lot sooner too.

I don't even remember when I first realized I could sing, or more importantly, when my father first realized I could. It was probably in church. I was raised as a Catholic and Catholics are unfortunately forced to sing way too high at mass every Sunday. God created altos, mezzo-sopranos, and sopranos, but you wouldn't know it from the sounds emanating from most choir lofts! Every song is written for a soprano. Man, that hurts your vocal cords when that's not your natural range. When I go to church now, which is infrequently, I am so self-conscious about my singing because despite my accomplishments in the music business, I'm not an opera singer. That just ain't my thing. One of these days I'm convinced that some parishioner is going to turn from her seat in the pew in front of me and ask, "Do you actually think you can sing?" And to that, I will proudly reply, "Only in God's eyes."

Unfortunately, these highly melodically structured hymns, along with my family's favorite popular ballads and songs, many of which were from Broadway musicals such as *The King and I*, *Annie Get Your Gun*, and *Flower Drum Song*, became the catalog of music that I would have to perform on command anytime and anywhere. When my father began asking me to sing at family functions, I did not like it at all. I would instantly go into a six-year-old's version of a panic attack. While I loved singing, I hated performing. Something about being onstage for all to see deeply frightened me.

My father, being quite an accomplished and driven man himself, would hear none of that. He enjoyed being in the limelight, as his later career in politics would prove. My reluctance to shine made him put me on the spot even more relentlessly. We would be enjoying a lovely meal when all of a sudden we'd hear the tapping of my father's spoon against his glass. When he had everyone's attention, he'd announce that I would be singing Bette Midler's "The Rose" (the only song we both liked) or "Getting to Know You" (my grandpa John's favorite song). Despite my embarrassment, I was the dutiful daughter who did what I was told. No child wants to disappoint her parents, or worse, think that she is the cause of friction between them. My parents, who were a classic example of opposites attracting, were already prone to fighting, so I felt pressed not to add to their tensions. But even after

I sang, they'd invariably argue, sometimes publicly, as my mother told my dad to leave me alone and my father ignored her. In fact, this would often make him push me more. He'd tell me that I was wasting my gift by not sharing it.

This torture went on for years at charity dinners, local political fund-raising events, and especially at family gatherings. I would spit out my food midbite when my father would surprise everyone, including me, with an announcement that I would be performing shortly. The worst was at our country club where we were the token Italian Albanians. He'd sneak over to the accordion and upright bass players and ask them to encourage me to sing with them. But my nerves were most frayed when he would tell me in advance that I was going to have to sing. I would barely sleep the night before. Then I'd spend the whole time in the bathroom warming up until they called for my performance. I hated the fact that every event that should have been great fun for a little kid was somehow tainted with anxiety. All I focused on when I was up in front of an audience (even one filled with loving family and friends) was the prospect of messing up. I was a perfectionist seeking approval. All that mattered was that I did a good job in my mind and in others', namely my dad's. It felt too much like I was in a dog-and-pony show. Naturally, I ended up resenting my father and my voice until one day I just stopped singing. Now, of course, I can acknowledge that in many ways, my father's insistence actually prepared me for the most stressful, on-the-spot gig ever—*Idol*! But back then, I had simply resolved never to be a singer, ever. I ceased loving music, and sadly enough, I ceased dreaming about a career in it, too. I remember looking in the bathroom mirror and asking God to take my voice away. Thankfully, God doesn't answer all of our prayers.

At around age nine or ten, I made the transition from wanting to be a singer to being a totally obsessed consumer of pop music. I found my first Top 40 station where all the big hits were played. It was on this station each weekend that Casey Kasem hosted the Top 40 countdown. I would wait by my tape recorder armed with a blank cassette, ready to hear my favorite songs after the ridiculously long commercial breaks. Church always over-lapped with the last few hits in the countdown, so I would beg my parents to tune in on the way to mass. It was painful to know that I wouldn't have a copy of Blondie's "Call Me" or Michael Jackson's "Rock with You" to hear all week long. You see, when I played music, I didn't *play* it, I looped it until everyone, including myself, was sick of it. I was a junkie for the emotion—the highs and lows I got from a song. I would sit on my bedroom floor for hours and just feel. It opened up a channel inside me. It spoke to me in ways my parents and friends at the time couldn't. When the radio was on, I knew all the words to every song and would annoy everyone around me with my endless singing. One day my friends and I were listening to Michael Jackson's "Human Nature." The song always made me feel the heavy in his heart, as if he was crying in the chorus. As I sang along, everyone made fun of how serious I looked when I got to that part. I was actually interpreting the sadness in it. I did not know then that Steve Porcaro, the lead keyboard-ist from the rock band Toto, had written the song for his daughter Heather after an uncomfortable incident at school. I was instinctively understanding the language of the chords and the melodies. You can't teach that. You either got *feel* or you don't.

By high school, my dad was no longer asking me to sing as much as he used to, thankfully. I think he got the message that I wasn't into him sin-gling me out in this way and he was tired of fighting with me and my mom about it anyway. But when he eased off me, singing became an interesting prospect again. I contemplated joining choir at school, but mistakenly tried out for the school's premier singing group instead. It was called Dohters, but the sign announcing auditions outside the music center didn't distinguish between their tryouts and the choir's. I wandered in and sang a song or two. The group was pretty much run by students and they were all impressed by my voice. They asked me to come back for the second round of auditions, but I was just a freshman then and knew nothing about the group or how prestigious it was to be part of it, so I blew it off. Needless to say, the senior members were not happy about that and would later use the excuse that I didn't blend in when I tried out again more seriously in my sophomore and junior years. Note to Reader: When someone tells you that you don't blend in, rush toward them and give them a great big hug, as they have just paid you the highest compliment you will ever receive. The goal in life is to stand out, *not* to blend in. And if I could speak to my fifteen-year-old self with the wisdom I possess now, I'd have it out with her for *ever* having gotten so upset over a comment like that.

Being told by my peers that my voice did not fit in with their rivaled another disastrous moment in my life that made me never want to set foot onstage again. This event occurred a few years earlier, on the day of my confirmation, when I was asked to perform on the church altar. I had practiced religiously with the organist, but at the last possible moment the music teacher decided to go all hip and switched to playing the guitar. For whatever reason, that threw me off and I sang in the wrong key because I couldn't find the right notes. I was completely out of tune. The parish office called my parents to say that I didn't have to return to the church to sing during the second ceremony later that day. They thought I should just stay home and enjoy my party. I swear the whole thing was a fluke. Nothing like that had ever happened before, but when the church doesn't even want you to sing, you know you're really in trouble. So between these two events, I was doubting my vocal abilities and letting my fears convince me that I should ignore my creative side. Once I abandoned that vital part of me, however, I was lost. The fact that I could sing made me different. Most days—with the exception of my confirmation day—it made me special. But like so many other kids at that stage of life, I didn't want to be different or special. I wanted to be like everyone else. Normal.

Reflections on Writing "Spinning Around" with Paula Abdul

Paula Abdul was at a pivotal place in her life when we met in 1998. The same was true of me. I had just lost my mother. Paula had just filed for divorce from her second husband and was using this experience to write songs about empowerment, loss, and moving on. That's where my head was at, too, so naturally we hit it off.

She had received a sampling of my music from a colleague of mine at *Billboard* magazine, where I was working at the time, and she reacted positively to the lyrical content. We scheduled a meeting during my lunch break. Can you imagine having only forty-five minutes, including travel time, for one of the most important dates of your life? Paula was already there when I arrived, which is funny because after that she was always late. I was often struck by how attractive she was in photographs but she looked even prettier in person. I immediately felt self-conscious in the combination of my Easy Spirit pumps (they always got me crosstown and back in under twenty minutes) and the vintage leather jacket I had bought in the East Village to give some edge to my very corporate Ann Taylor shirt. The whole outfit was a cross between what you'd find on the racks at T.J. Maxx and in Joan Jett's closet during her "I Love Rock 'n Roll" heyday. Not hot!

I don't know what Paula saw in me. Maybe she could sense that I was in flux just like she was—trying to find something to hold on to, to center me, to stop the pain of my mother's death. Whatever it was, she looked past the fact that I was in advertising sales and honed in on my creative abilities. She asked me to write with her, and for that I will be forever grateful.

One of Paula's greatest qualities is that she is very giving and unguarded. So much so that she sometimes finds herself surrounded by the scavengers of the earth. Enter the just-released-from-prison cowriter who somehow convinced Paula that he could give her the hit song she needed.

There we were, all in a room together—ex-con, star, and ad sales rep at *Billboard* by day/wannabe artist by night. If anyone had been watching, they would have thought that Paula was being punk'd. We hardly seemed like three of the four people responsible for making a number one hit in the UK called "Spinning Around." I actually knew this person before I met Paula and had witnessed him trying to smooth-talk $60K out of my brother's best friend for a partnership and piece of his music business that according to my brother's friend ended up yielding no return on his investment. As far as I could see, it got this guy a fat new loft to live/work in and to shag girls in. (Warning to the Wise: Don't ever invest in the music business if you are not *in* the music business. You might as well take your money and burn it. But if you choose to ignore this tip and invest anyway, then at least find someone who is qualified to advise you.)

This cowriter was brutal. He yelled and screamed at me. I think I even cried. "No, it's not a hit chorus," he determined, even though he had never written one. A hit chorus was the last thing I was worried about. I was trying to stay true to Paula's story. She was "trading in her sorrow for some joy that [she'd] borrowed from back in the day." Girlfriend, I could totally relate. She "threw out all [her] old clothes, got [herself] a better wardrobe, [she had] something to say." Holla, girl. I needed some new shit, too.

I had truly found a partner in crime. Someone who was going through what I was going through. I wasn't going to let Paula down by abandoning the frank conversations we had had about our lives and current situations. Especially the part about "did I forget to mention that I found a new direction and it leads back to me?" That's right—we were searching for ourselves: not who we thought we were but who we *really* were. We were on a mission, we were spinning around, so motherfuckers had better get out of our way. What we would both find out is that only one person is ever really in your way, and that's yourself.

The time I spent with Paula was priceless. Shortly after "Spinning Around," she moved me into her apartment in West Hollywood for a month. I think she sensed that I was a regular girl who could be privy to the inner workings of her life and still be trusted to keep that knowledge to myself. Of course, she could count on me. I mean, who the hell did I know? I think she felt safe and when you're that famous, finding someone who won't betray your confidence is like money in the bank. We spent every single hour of every single day together, laughing, crying, writing, and getting massages. We were the best of friends for that brief time. She turned me on to more beauty potions and lotions than I ever knew existed. Everything about her was fabulous. Her apartment was full of silks and satins. Her walk-in closets were meticulously lined with designer clothes and her medicine cabinets were filled with the best in skin-care products. It was a product junkie's paradise.

I believe that things don't just happen to you. God, coincidence, and fate all play their part. But you also need luck. My father once shared the greatest saying of all time with me and I have sworn by it since: "Luck is where opportunity meets preparation." And he could not have been more right. It was luck that led me to Paula, but I was also ready for that luck. Ready to make a jump. Ready to be heard. I had at least four hundred unpublished songs to my name at the time. Clearly, I had spent endless hours honing my craft and getting to know myself, so I could recognize and empathize with others' feelings. Together, we empowered each other and that's what "Spinning Around" was all about. It represented our hope for the future and letting go of the past.

We both had bright destinies ahead of us. But Paula was on the verge of hitting it really big again, and we heard the news two years before anyone else. I had never put much faith in psychics. I knew a few of them from various hotlines because my brother had run up a sizable phone bill asking if our mom would be okay when she was sick. Due to the circumstances, I'd tried to get our money back, but clearly they saw that coming because they never took any of my calls. Dolores Cardelucci was different. She had a real gift. She scared the hell out of me when I first met her. As you can tell by her name, she was Italian. And she was seriously off-putting at first. She almost barked at you until she read your present and future circumstances. Once she had a sense of what was going on in your life, she softened and was lovely. Paula went in for a session and came out saying that Dolores thought she was too emotional for a full reading, but that she was going to be on a television show shortly and her career would be hotter than ever. I thought to myself, *This lady is nuts. Paula is an artist not an actress.* What did I know? Two years later, just as Dolores had predicted, Paula would be on *American Idol* and I would have two number one singles under my belt. By then, we had spun off in our own directions only to collide again down the road. I would never have guessed that our paths would intersect the way they did. And believe me, neither did Paula.

Two

SOBER

"I'm safe, up high, nothing can touch me,

so why do I feel this party's over?

No pain inside, you're my protection.

so how do I feel this good sober?"

s far as addictions go, having an eating disorder is definitely one of the least glamorous and in some ways the most isolating. I mean, would you ever call up your friends and tell them to get ready because you had a big night planned at the grocery store? What a blast it will be! We'll all go to the baked goods section, stock up on way too many Hostess Twinkies and Ho Hos, crawl up on the couch wearing our fat jeans, and stuff our faces until we fall asleep from the sugar coma. Then comes the real fun in the morning, when we'll wake up in a haze and beat ourselves up 'cause we gained five pounds; which will take a week or two to lose.

Drugs and booze benders in the music business often involve fabulous people and late nights in the chicest of clubs, five-star hotels, and yachts. My eating binges, however, usually involved a car, a supermarket parking lot, and a broken streetlamp so no one would recognize me. But all three diseases have one thing in common: shame.

I was a thin kid. I was never picky about what I ate, but I LOVED junk food. Anything chocolate had my name written all over it. A bag of cookies for dinner sounded like the perfect meal to me; especially since my mother, God rest her soul, could not cook to save her life. I remember having my high school soccer team over for dinner one evening and she made us escarole and pancakes. We were up all night fighting for the bathroom. Unfortunately, I think I inherited my culinary gene from her.

Much to other people's understandable annoyance, as an adolescent I could eat everything in sight and never gain weight. Of course, that would change later in life, but no one—least of all me—knew that then. My first job in high school was in a candy-and-gelato shop where there were vats of melted chocolate in the storage closet that I would dip a Styrofoam cup into and drink from, straight up. I was in heaven and never thought twice about calories. I didn't even know what they were. In fact, the owner of the shop would often say that I was his best salesperson because there was a visible shift in inventory when I was working. Yeah, from the shelves to my stomach. He really should have checked the sales receipts.

During the summer before college, a friend went to "fat camp," a place where teens would go to lose weight. She wasn't that heavy, so I never understood why she went, but she came back looking great and that made me think that maybe I should lose some weight, too. So I followed a strict diet plan that included watching what I ate for six days straight, then "pigging out" on Sundays, when I would eat whatever I wanted. I kind of enjoyed controlling my food and counting calories. It gave me power over my life at a time when I had begun feeling powerless. It was around then that I began realizing I was different from most of the kids I knew, even though I seemingly fit in. I was bored by sports, aimlessly hanging around, and many other things that define teenage years. By my last year of high school, I had finally been accepted into Dohters, but my voice definitely overpowered everyone else's and I often felt the need to stifle it so I wouldn't call so much attention to myself or alienate others. To me, having a gift like singing was a lot like getting an ice cream maker for Christmas. You're thankful for it, but you stuff it in the closet because you have no idea what to do with it. It's nice, but impractical.

As the results of my diet became evident, people started remarking about how great I looked. Guys especially. I thought to myself, *Wait, did I not look good before?* All of a sudden I was scrutinizing my body. A whole new obsession was introduced into my life. I had devised a game plan to help manage it and it all hinged on what the scale said. In the morning, if the red pointer indicated that I had maintained my goal weight of 116 pounds or less, then I was okay and I allowed myself to have a good day free of negative thoughts. If it indicated that I weighed more than 116 pounds, I was a loser, beating myself up, restricting my food intake even more, and wanting to fast-forward to the next morning, when I could redeem myself by returning to my perfect weight. Before breakfast, I wouldn't allow myself so much as a drop of water until after stepping on the scale, for fear that I would be an ounce over 116 pounds. Some days I would step on it ten times to see what my fluctuations were during the course of twelve hours. Everything revolved around that ideal number. It represented my worth. I wasted so many moments living for when I would be "thin." I wish I could get them back.

As you can imagine, eating only 1,000 calories six days a week was really tough. I was constantly starving and longing for my big "pig-out day" when I would gorge on sweets. I'd dream about all the chocolate milk shakes and brownies I'd be eating and could hardly wait for 12 A.M. on Sunday morning when, technically, the feast would begin. It was like the Last Supper every week. The problem was, it became harder and harder to limit myself during those six days in between and I would sometimes go over 1,000 calories. If I did, I would say screw it and start eating whatever I wanted (which sometimes amounted to 5,000 or 6,000 calories daily) and then I'd deny myself even more during the next twenty-four hours to compensate. This started a pattern of dieting for two days and then bingeing for one. (Any Italian will tell you that food is everything, so there is no way I would have ever considered throwing up. In my culture, bulimia is a mortal sin.)

Soon, my body was completely confused by the influx of sugar. It caused an immediate high, followed by such a devastating low, that every fiber of my being began jonesing for something to help avoid the inevitable crash. My body needed sugar like a drug addict needs drugs and I became completely out of control. This manifested in night bingeing where I would wake up three or four times before dawn and stuff my face. I would sneak downstairs like a thief, with my heart racing, and I'd stand in front of the refrigerator devouring everything in sight, praying not to be caught and feeling totally ashamed. Throughout my twenties, I was a walking Pac woman chomping my way through friends' refrigerators all over the country. My consumptions included the top of a wedding cake and a Thanksgiving pie the night *before* Thanksgiving. I did manage to leave some things uneaten, though, like the dead cat I once found stored in someone's freezer—they were waiting until the ice outside thawed so they could bury her. Odd, I know.

During my sophomore year in college, I was caught in the cycle of fighting to get back down to 116 pounds (I probably weighed 145 at my high point) and surrendering to the overwhelming cravings. I wouldn't take trips to the beach or go on spring breaks with my friends because I hated the way I looked. All I ever thought about was food, my weight, and counting calories incessantly in my head the way an accountant runs numbers. I also thought about how everyone around me was thin and I wasn't. Note: I am *not* saying that 145 pounds is heavy—I'm saying that it didn't fit my ridiculous notion of perfect at the time, so please don't be offended by this number.

Of course, depression was inevitable. I would sleep for hours in my dorm room, wishing the day away so that morning would come again and I could start my calorie counter over, getting it right this time. I was miserable. I didn't want anyone to see me or touch me. I honestly can't remember much from 1988 to 1992. I walked around my college campus like a zombie with just enough strength to pull myself together for class and not ruin my chances of getting into a decent grad school—the next rung on the ladder of success I'd set out for myself to climb. I was not the person then that I am today. I was lost; I was sick and I very much wanted to disappear.

I let no one into this darkness. I just wallowed in it until finally I realized that I had to figure out what was going on inside of me, or what was the point of living? Addictions don't come from out of the blue. They are signs that something internally is not right. That something, for me, was my continuing effort to be someone I wasn't. Ever since my childhood, I had been denying that I could sing, denying that I could hear melodies in my head day and night, and denying that music was a real career option. I was listening to my mother's fears that music was a poor man's pursuit and that it would never lead me to marriage and a stable home life. I was rebelling against my father's dominance as he pushed me on stage to perform against my will so many times before. On top of that, I had my own perfection issues and was suffering from low self-esteem and attaching my worth to my weight gain or loss. Pounds were real numbers I could put a value on, and obsessing about my weight kept my focus off finding myself.

At this point, I had no idea what I wanted to do or where I wanted to be. I only knew that where I was wasn't making me happy. Duke, the school I attended, was a big university, and while not all the kids there acted like clones of their predominantly rich conservative parents, too many of the ones that crossed my path did. I can't tell you how many times I heard one of my classmates say, "My daddy's a lawyer, so I'm going take over his practice." I was also disheartened by how many women I knew seemed to be in school only to find wealthy partners to marry. What the hell? It was 1990! I wanted to shout at them, "Create your own damn life!"

What I know now is that all too often the qualities people loathe in others are the ones they're fighting in themselves. It may be that I singled out these types of students among the many thousands because they hinted at what I could become if I continued to let myself be influenced by others' ambitions for me. I think subconsciously I imagined I might someday turn into a clone of them more than I would become my own person.

During the summer of 1991, my night bingeing had reached an all-time high. I was so sleep deprived I could barely get through the day. I was hiding pizza boxes under my bed, and whenever my father would find them, he would go ballistic, telling me that I had to stop eating so much. He had completely underestimated what a real problem I had. Probably because he feared that my issues were a reflection of his and my mother's unstable relationship and its emotional effects on me and my brother, and he couldn't bear to shoulder some of the responsibility.

Our insurance didn't cover psychiatrist visits, so I decided to check myself into a hospital in Florida. I would be covered for a month of intense therapy. What I didn't realize was that I had been admitted to a psych ward. The doors had to be left open at all times and I could not leave the floor unless I was supervised. The smell of chlorine in the hallways and the fluorescent lights made it impossible to trick myself into thinking I was anywhere else but a hospital. The other patients were mostly binge eaters like me, but shared horror stories about their fathers and brothers raping them. These stories must have tapped into the reality of my own childhood molestation at the hands of a young family friend, and they made me very uncomfortable. Clearly, though, I wasn't ready to deal with that yet. I wanted to bolt from there as fast as I could, but if I left early I would be out of pocket for the few days I had been there already. I was screwed.

I think I accepted Jesus Christ into my life during my stay just so that I could go jogging around the hospital grounds. Taking the Lord into your life was the head nurse's condition for letting us leave the floor. While her real vocation might have been tending to the sick, she took the job of converting her patients into born-again Christians just as seriously. I definitely wanted to be born again . . . but as another person.

My brief stint in the psych ward made it impossible to eat at night, so I naturally lost some weight. But the urges and the cravings did not go away and I was back into bingeing almost as soon as I left, which made me feel even more like shit. But throughout it all, I began to realize that my issues were deeper than food. I was unhappy. *Truly* unhappy. I didn't like myself at all. But thankfully, that would change.

It's not like I went away to the desert and prayed for three months and then the answer came to me. Or that I was hallucinating on acid when I had my epiphany. Instead it was really a combination of events that occurred when I returned to college for my final semesters that helped me find my path again.

Duke was known for its Final Fours. It's a big basketball school, so naturally people came from all over the country to watch the games. Fans would flock to the student center before, during, and after these games to buy school shirts and paraphernalia to take home as souvenirs.

One day, while I was in my performing arts class, which was uncharacteristically being held in the student center, I witnessed a visitor, who was with his three-year-old child, start to heave and throw up blood. Of course, the child began wailing. It was a frightening thing for anyone to see, so I can only imagine what this toddler was feeling. Some of my classmates and I rushed over to help. It was an agonizing thirty minutes before an ambulance came. And during that time, it struck me that not one other student who passed by stopped to see how they might help. They just kept moving along, heading to wherever it was they were headed as if no one else existed. I suppose that kids anywhere can be self-absorbed, and that the same indifference could have occurred in any office building or on any street corner in America. But it didn't happen in any of those places. It happened at my school and it happened in front of me. And in that moment I realized that I could not see myself ever becoming so single-minded about getting ahead in life that I could be so oblivious to another person in need. Were these kids so self-involved? Had they become so entitled that they didn't even recognize a fucking tragedy when they saw one?! How could they just walk on by? I vowed right then and there never to be like them. NEVER to be so programmed by my goals that I lost my soul.

The man died shortly after the ambulance arrived, and I often think that if he were alive today, I would thank him for helping me realize that *direction without heart means nothing*. Success is not only about money and status but about being the best person you can be in all areas of your life. I was far from being at my best, but I sure as hell was struggling to get there. This event crystallized my goals for me. In fact, looking back, I realize that this experience helped influence the choices I made when my mother later became ill with ovarian cancer. I had to decide: Was I going to ignore the fact that she was dying and carry on with my own life? Or was I going to stop and do the right thing? But even before then—on that day at the student center as I stood there disappointed in my own peers' lapse of humanity—the question I had to answer for myself was: Am I going to be like everyone else or do I have the guts to be me? The guts to be different? The guts to be a singer if I want to?

It wasn't until the spring of 1992, during my last semester at Duke, that I would finally decide to throw caution to the wind and reawaken my long-lost dreams. The first step I took was to admit to myself and others that I did not want to be a lawyer (an occupation I had felt that everyone could approve of and flaunt like a new car or engagement ring). No, instead I wanted to be a singer like Mariah Carey, my idol at the time. I was enthralled by "Vision of Love " from her debut album. And the final push that spurred me to make this leap of faith occurred while house-sitting for a professor named Kristine Stiles. Ms. Stiles had entrusted the well-being of her two cats to my longtime friend Anne while she was away, meaning that Anne was to stay at Ms. Stiles's house to watch, feed, and play with them. Anne had neglected to mention her violent allergies to cats for fear that it would affect her good graces with the professor. Hence, without Ms. Stiles's knowledge, I got the job, and it was a good thing I did. I loved waking up in her town house with all of its bright and beautiful artwork. It was such a far contrast to my drab dorm room, which had become more like a prison for me, that I found myself feeling instantly alive. There was something about being away from campus, too, that allowed me to feel hope again. I still don't know Ms. Stiles, and will probably never have the opportunity to meet her, but I bet if I asked her about her life, she would say that she followed her heart, which led her to a career in the arts. I could certainly feel that in her home, and her evident passions opened my heart and mind up to a realm of possibilities for me, too. I didn't have to be twenty pounds overweight, feeling like I didn't belong and wanting to sleep my life away. I didn't have to be what anyone else expected me to be—a lawyer, doctor, or some other "dignified" professional. I could now close my eyes and ask myself what I truly wanted to be, even if I wasn't sure it was possible, and I could also honestly accept the answer, which was that I unequivocally wanted to be a singer.

When I first came to that realization, it was like a light went on in my head. I knew I had to finish school, not because I wanted to, but because I instinctively knew that the experience would help me. My education was my insurance policy in case my plans went awry. What I didn't know then is that this university, which I rebelled against so fiercely, would be the key to securing my first job in the music business. I had finally acknowledged my dream and given it the power it deserved.

Reflections on Writing "Sober" with Pink

Meeting Pink was a career highlight for me, but admittedly it was not at all what I had expected. In 2006 I was at the top of my game, having written successful songs with the biggest superstars on the planet. I had become the "go-to girl" for labels in search of hits for their pop artists. Shortly after Pink turned in *I'm Not Dead*, the president of her record label, Clive Davis, had suggested she add a few more songs to the mix before choosing what would become the final album. Of course, hitting the charts big is a numbers game. Sometimes, the more material you write for an album, the more likely you are to find that hit single . . . or several hit singles. Alecia (which is her real name and the name by which she introduced herself) didn't need anyone to write more music with her for that album as she had already penned the chart-toppers "Who Knew" and "U + Ur Hand." Nevertheless, I was asked to work with her and I was extremely excited to do so. By all accounts, she was a one-of-a-kind talent.

When she came to the studio in Culver City where I was working alongside producer/writer Greg Wells, I immediately sensed something was off. She seemed guarded, which made my walls come right up, too. In her defense, it's not easy to hear that the record you've worked on for the last twelve months could use a few more songs . . . and by the way, there's some girl you don't know yet out there who can help you. I can just imagine her saying, "What fucking girl?" That girl would, of course, be me. Even though we had met in the dead of summer, there was a chill in the studio that day. We wrote two songs together, but I can't say there was an immediate chemistry. I suspected that she wasn't dying over the work we did—or over me, for that matter. One of the songs, "No One Else," ultimately went on Allison Iraheta's debut album. I came up with the start of that song after hearing Pink talk about her relationship with her husband. I should have known to let her take the lead with the ideas, as it was her album. She had all the good ones anyway, especially when it came to telling her own story. I thought I'd played it wrong and left the studio feeling like I hadn't delivered. In a million years I never thought I'd hear from her again.

A little over a year later I got a call from her manager, Roger Davies, who said that Alecia wanted me to work with her on another song. I definitely thought he had called me by mistake, but I wasn't going to be the one to tell him that. I was thrilled at the prospect of working with her again. As chance would have it, my session the next day had been cancelled, so of course I went to see her in Malibu, where she was recording.

I was nervous. It had been weird between us the last time we worked together and I don't like bullshitting, so I knew we needed to get to a place where we could discuss what had happened. We had both been going through a lot of other stuff at that time. I knew Pink was an amazing artist, but I needed to bond with her as a person. It would have been easy to let that discomfort lie there, to blow it off and just push through the session. Especially since I don't like confrontation, but I thought, *Wouldn't it serve us better to have a relationship based on honesty? How could* we *write a song about truth if we were lying to each other?* Once we talked it all out, there was a feeling of intimacy between us. I think, we felt safer being vulnerable around each other, and safety was something it seemed like we both craved in the studio because it's one of the places where we really let go. Once we knew where the other was coming from, we could move past the issues left over from before. In my opinion, women can be their own worst enemies. We constantly throw each other under the bus. I am guilty of it sometimes as well, but I am committed to stopping. If you have a problem with another woman, tell her. We owe it to each other to be our best support system and not take each other down. Men don't do that shit. And when you work through something with a woman, the bond is infinitely deeper.

Now, you have to imagine that all this chick bonding is going down with some red wine and way too many cigarettes, so when it comes time to write "Sober," I am bombed, three sheets to the wind. Normally one or two drinks and I am ready to dance on a table or in the middle of the street. (I am the epitome of a lightweight.)

So, here we are writing "Sober" and I am anything but that. What followed was the best game of drunken tennis I have ever played. I would say a line and she'd come back with something better and then I would be like, "Okay, well, what've you got for this?" We were challenging each other—stretching and pulling from our experiences. All of a sudden having had an eating disorder was coming in handy. I could relate to how a drug of choice, whether it be alcohol, drugs, sex, or food, numbs the pain inside and makes it easier to cope. We made one another better—or rather, I should just speak for myself: *she* made *me* better—and it turned out to be one of the best writing sessions of my life.

Not one artist, other than Pink, has ever told me to shut up when their vocals were being recorded, and she was right to do so. She can sing her ass off and doesn't need any direction in recording a vocal that captures the sentiment of the song. She's the Janis Joplin of today and is one of the best out there. Writing with her was a definitive highlight in my career and as I left there that night—or really, as I pulled over on the side of Pacific Coast Highway to be sure I was okay enough to drive—I realized that I had worked with greatness. When it came to being an artist, she was one for all the reasons that I wasn't during my twenties. She knew herself completely and was able to express her unique point of view clearly and consistently in her music. It took me longer to find my center, and by the time I did, I had discovered that I was more suited to being a songwriter who remained behind the scenes than a performing artist. I had ended up with the right job. Pink affirmed that for me.

I am convinced that the decision I made that fateful semester in college to pursue music, and to put my emotions and feelings into songs ever since then, really saved my life. With each new tune that I wrote, I got to know myself more and more. I was able to finally face the feelings that had not only been stuffed far down inside of me but had also made me sick. Each song helped me breathe easier, and the healing came because I was no longer denying what hurt.

I sensed that there were others out there who struggled with addictions, too, and who might find the same comfort I found through creativity. In 2007 I created, with the help of West LA Music, Taxi, and other contributors, a recording studio at the Lake View Terrace Phoenix House in California. My father had been on the board of Phoenix House, a drug rehab center, for much of his life and he asked me to contribute. I have never been crazy about giving money to charities because it's hard to know how much of the proceeds go to the actual cause. I'd much rather help a friend or respond directly to someone in need. But I convinced Phoenix House to let me build these studios and control the budgets so I could ensure that the money I was investing was going where it was supposed to. To their credit, the organization agreed and three more studios like the first one have since been built in Yorktown, New York; Austin, Texas; and Citra, Florida.

Music allows people to download their emotions and address them head-on. It's the best therapy I never paid for. I meet kids in recovery all the time who were incredibly withdrawn before they got a chance to work in the studio. Kids who have withheld their personal stories from their counselors for six months or longer until music helped them open up. Given one week of recording, these same kids are writing and singing profoundly honest songs about their personal experiences. Songs about hating their mother because she left them or feeling so horrible inside that they want to die. Music helps us find our truth and discover ourselves. If you are not musically inclined, a journal can work in a similar way. Pour your heart out and don't edit what you write. Read it back and get to know yourself, your true uncensored self. I like telling artists to write down words that really communicate who they are. Artists need to stand for something that distinguishes them from everyone else. But artists are not the only people who can benefit from this type of self-examination. Everyone can, and the key to success is knowing yourself well enough to tell the difference between what gets your soul off and what kills it. STAY AWAY FROM WHAT KILLS IT!

Three

TAKING CHANCES

"What do you say to taking chances?
What do you say to jumping off the edge? And
never knowing if there's solid ground below
or a hand to hold or hell to pay,
What do you say?"

Announcing to my parents in 1992 when I graduated from college that I wanted to be a professional singer was like telling them that I had flushed the hundred-thousand-plus dollars they spent on my education down the toilet. I hadn't made the distinction yet between being a singer and an artist, but even if I had gotten the nuances right, the news still wouldn't have gone over very well. Especially with my mom, who thought that all musicians were drug addicts. By the way, drug addicts, to my parents, were people who smoked marijuana. Thankfully, my mother had never heard of hard drugs like coke or heroin, which, in my experience, are the more likely drugs of choice for the music crowd. The other images of musicians she harbored were equally stereotypical and unflattering. She thought of them as broke, tattooed, and, more often than not, from the wrong side of the tracks. She wanted me to marry into a good family, to have a man support me and give me the life she had wanted for herself. A man from Duke University would have fit the bill, but it was a little late for that since my only true love affair in college was with my bed and any simple carbs I could get my hands on. Yes, I slept with wild abandon and never scheduled a class before noon because I woke up daily in a stupor from a sugar crash. It always took a few hours for the haze to wear off. While other girls might have been husband-seeking collegians, I was a certifiable food slut.

So I did what every struggling singer and actress does when faced with unemployment. I became a waitress, which, considering my food issues, actually seemed like an obvious yet somewhat dangerous choice. I had an entire walk-in refrigerator full of pies and cakes to choose from. The other upside was that between the three different restaurants I was working at, I was making serious cash for someone my age. Being a waitress was actually great training for working with artists. The first order of business was always to size up the clients and figure out what they would respond to (humor, intelligence, craziness) so that I could get a 20 percent tip, or, in the case of artists, a real shot at a cut on their album. Surprisingly enough, I was getting more of a handle on my food addiction during that period. Dedicating my energy to succeeding at something I loved to do was a huge motivating factor in confronting some of my more self-destructive behavior. That and the fact that these restaurants had serious rules about snacking (or "stealing," as they called it) and served less than four-star fare to the waitstaff!

While I was all gung ho on my new career path, it soon dawned on me that I really didn't know anybody in the music business, except, of course, the late, great Ahmet Ertegun, the head of Atlantic Records at the time, whom I had met briefly right before I graduated high school and whose house my family stayed at when we went to Turkey during the prior summer.

Yes, that's exactly how the mind of everyone who wants to be a singer works. Combing the recesses of our memories, we all hope to find someone— anyone—who can help us get that first big break. Given who my "in" was, one would have thought I'd hit the jackpot. My dad, who had become a U.S. congressman from New York by then, had told Ahmet that he had a teenage daughter who could sing. He even convinced him to let me use Atlantic studios to record some demos that my wonderful, talented aunt Doni had written. My dad's aim was to see if his pushing me to sing as a kid had been justified. My hope was to get Ahmet's professional opinion and that it would free me from the harsh words of my Dohters peers and the church.

I had also hoped he'd encourage me to record an album for Atlantic Records. The only challenge to my plan was that this all happened at the same time that Debbie Gibson was reigning at Atlantic, so the songs written by my aunt, called "Reckless Motorcycle Rider" and "Love Is the Answer," didn't stand a chance against Debbie's self-penned "Out of the Blue" and "Only in My Dreams." When I finally got to have my ten-minute meeting with Ahmet, he said, "Kid, you have a very good voice, but stay in school." Needless to say, I was crushed, and this incident became another reason in the sea of reasons for me to turn my back on my creativity. I should thank him, though, because I included the music I recorded at Atlantic studios in my college application and it helped me get into Duke, where I was recruited to study opera. On my arrival, I was horrified at how rigid and uninspiring operatic voice lessons seemed to me. I guess I instinctively knew that my voice was more of a vehicle for my soul than an instrument to be trained. On top of that, the music building was located on the east campus, a place where the in-crowd said all the artsy weirdos lived. Little did I know they were talking about me.

Years later I ran into Mr. Ertegun at an industry event where he was being honored. Of course, when I approached him, he didn't remember our brief encounter in the days when I was "Kara, the teenaged aspiring singer." He only knew me as "Kara the songwriter" who was now taking the music industry by storm. The guy was eighty years old by then, so what was I gonna do, chide him for not seeing my potential back in high school? Not if there was a chance I could stay at his house again. I never did return to his seaside retreat in Turkey, but I did join the Warner Music Group (which houses Atlantic Records) as a record executive. How ironic is that?

Other than Mr. Ertegun, who didn't seem to be the likeliest person to ask another favor of after his first take on my talent, I had no idea how to break into the music industry. I had read a story about Mariah Carey giving her demo tape to Tommy Mottola at a party, but I didn't have a tape (other than the one from high school) and I certainly didn't travel in the same circles as the top music executives. So I spent my time dreaming about meeting Mr. Mottola while steaming the wine glasses and polishing the silverware at the restaurant where I worked.

In order to put a demo tape together that would effectively showcase my voice, I knew I had to select some really great original songs. But that proved to be challenging because I didn't know any songwriters either. Truth be told, I didn't even know that was a real occupation. And when I started to meet some of these songwriters, they weren't exactly inclined to give their babies away to an unknown singer who still lived with her parents.

At around the same time as I was struggling to find an entrée into the business, I was fielding calls from friends about all their exciting new jobs. My best friend in the whole world, Suzie Paxton, was going to compete as a fencer in the Olympics; others were hired at top investment banking firms and were well on their way to earning gajillions, and of course there were the ones who had just gotten accepted into great medical, law, or business schools. My proudest accomplishment to date was getting the weekend night shifts at the eateries that employed me, which was a huge step up from the afternoon shift, where all the sweet blue-haired ladies who lunch needed me to read their bills and still only tipped a dollar. I loved them anyway because they reminded me of my nanny Mary. Whenever anyone, outside of close friends and family, inquired about what I was doing, there was always a moment of silence that seemed to swallow me whole before I would say, "Well, I'm working on my music."

"Music? What do you mean, music? You sing?" most of them asked. "Yes," I would always shyly reply, acknowledging how crazy it sounded when you said it aloud.

Then came the inevitable and much-dreaded question: "How are you going to make a living doing that?" I had no quick answer, but I sure as hell was gonna figure it out.

Ironically, now that I've made it in the music business, I'm considered the coolest person they know, especially by their kids who love all the artists I work with.

One of the people calling to catch up was a woman named Mary Bentley Houk, with whom I went to college. We were friends but I wouldn't say that we were overly close. Her biggest problem was keeping weight on, while mine was not killing her from envy when she'd confide her frustration about it with her third piece of pizza in hand. She had moved from Atlanta, Georgia, to Greenwich, Connecticut (about twenty minutes from where I lived in Westchester), to work for her aunt's husband at a gourmet fish company. She eventually left that job when her southern debutante ways and her uncle's hard-core New York edge clashed. She needed a place to crash. At the time my parents were getting separated and my mother was in the early stages of her long battle with cancer, so it was not the best time for a houseguest. I felt badly for her, so I convinced my parents to let her stay with us. As luck, or fate, would have it, she had befriended a woman who worked for the parent company of *Billboard* magazine, BPI Communications, while she was living with her aunt. Mary Bentley had found out about a job opening there and interviewed for the position of assistant to the publisher, Howard Lander, and editor in chief, Timothy White. She got the job and at the same time was offered another one at a textile company for $2,000 dollars more per year. Music or textiles? That was her dilemma. For me, it seemed like a no-brainer. Thankfully, she went for the money.

As soon as she mentioned that she was turning down the job at *Billboard*, it was as if I was hearing angels singing from heaven. Getting a position there would solve all my problems. I could spare my mother from the shame of admitting to her friends that after all my education and a shot at snagging some of the most eligible bachelors in the collegiate world, I was a waitress. More important, I would be learning about the business of music. It was perfect. I asked Mary Bentley to give them my name. I am forever indebted to her for doing so. I interviewed and got the job at the music magazine. I was an assistant, whatever that was. And I was closer than ever to my dream.

Note to Reader: When you're looking for a job in your industry of choice, it's really important to just get your foot in the door. This worked for me and for so many others as well. In fact, Jimmy Buffett worked in the mailroom at *Billboard* long before his success with "Margaritaville." If you work hard, the powers that be will notice you and you will get promoted. You will also have the chance to see what you like and don't like about that particular field. That sort of experience is truly invaluable.

Working as an assistant could have been a disaster for me, especially because I never liked authority. Even though I did well in school and didn't get into any real trouble, I had a major attitude problem when it came to being told what to do. I was once kicked out of camp for telling the counselors that my parents didn't spend $5,000 a summer for me to clean the bathrooms. If I was that counselor, I would have purposely clogged all the toilets after that comment and locked me in there. My first week on the job was extremely hectic because of some high-level internal meetings going on. I had to bring files over to the meeting site, but when I handed them to my main boss, Howard Lander, and a few of the other company bigwigs, he immediately asked me to stand in the corner and wait for him. I didn't like the sound of that. Nobody put "baby in the corner" and for a moment I wanted to quit until he came over and quietly told me to look at my blouse, which had somehow opened, revealing my bra and more of my boobs than I would have liked BPI's executive committee to see. Not a great first impression. I was mortified, but at least I understood why he'd given me a time-out. Maybe the music business was more buttoned up than my mother had thought after all.

Howard was particular about what he needed from an assistant but respectful, and I learned in time that if I speedily did what he asked me to do, he'd be happy. He was an incredible boss who was very understanding of my situation with my mother. In the three years I worked directly for him, he allowed me as much flexibility as possible so I could take her to the hospital, to doctor's appointments, for second opinions and chemo infusions. He would answer his own phone on days when I couldn't come in. He even granted me a leave of absence after one of her big operations.

Then there was this one time when I had to take my grandmother to the doctor. Howard had planned on being out that day, so I brought her to work with me and set her up in his office. I turned on the television to keep her entertained and shut the door, assuming no one would dare open it. But when I went to the bathroom, the head of sales entered the office to put some papers on Howard's desk and got the shock of his life. There on Howard's couch was my ninety-three-year-old nanny Mary. He immediately called Howard at home and asked if he knew that there was an elderly woman hanging out in his office. Luckily, Howard understood my predicament and let it slide.

My job was the one area of my life where I didn't feel like I was pushing a boulder up a mountain. I had an understanding boss who gave me access to the inner workings of the business side of music. I knew the names of every record label head, big managers, and publishers and slowly learned who the power players were, many of whom I now deal with today. It was an insider's education I could never have acquired at my university, or gotten from anyone but this man, who at times felt more like a father than my boss. He knew what was important in life; he valued family and made it easy for me to make mine a priority. It only made me want to do more for him. That lesson has stuck with me all these years. I always try to encourage my employees to take time to be with their sick family members and to take care of themselves, too, no matter how much stress it causes me. Howard taught me the invaluable lesson that being human should always come before being a boss.

My other compassionate boss was the late great Timothy White, who was a respected rock critic. He was very eccentric and wore a bow tie to the office every day. My main responsibility working for him was to transcribe his interviews for his weekly column, "Music to My Ears." To hear artists like Garth Brooks and Ricki Lee Jones talk about their lives and music was mind-blowing. Tim had a theory that all good music comes from great pain. I didn't understand what he meant until I started writing, but God, do I wish he was alive now so I could tell him how right he was. He believed that great artists could put that pain into words and music that was ultimately universal because of its relatable truth. He planted that seed in my head, and in doing so, I am sure that when I began writing, I knew I had to connect to my feelings, which has been the basis for most of the hit songs I have cowritten. Tim knew that the best music always comes from the heart.

By being his assistant I was exposed to artists and music I had never heard of—Cocteau Twins, the Story, even Alanis Morissette's first CD, *Jagged Little Pill*, six months before it came out. I was a pig in shit. I was getting my business education from Howard and my creative one from Tim. Looking back, I get goose bumps to think that perhaps I was predestined for this. (If you smush all the letters in my name together, the ones in the middle make me believe this, too: KaRADIOguardi.) Howard and Tim unknowingly gave me the tools that I would use to become successful long after working at *Billboard*. They were, up to that point, my best teachers in the school of music.

While I was learning so much at work, I was still having problems getting anybody to give me songs for my demo tape. A few months before starting at *Billboard*, I had decided to join a local rock coffeehouse band out of Ossining called Gramma Trips. I never did understand how we settled on that name. Someone was probably high (not me, as I was annoyingly way too square for that) and when they tripped over their grandmother or their grandmother tripped over them, the title just seemed kind of genius.

I was hired to be the chick singer, and that's just what they meant. I was supposed to look hot (which wasn't easy for a self-conscious suburban girl still battling with a few extra pounds), sing some riffs, and pretty much leave the writing and the management of the band to the guys. The pressure of having to look a certain way definitely made me anxious about my appearance. If I was going be serious about music, I knew I had to completely stop eating my emotions and start singing them. Plus, the bassist was super hot and loved to unbutton his shirt just enough to make the girls' imaginations run wild: and mine did. I loved being in the group. I was letting loose and doing what were for me crazy things like swimming in the Central Park Lake after gigs. More important, we got to play all kinds of different music like songs from the Band, the Beatles, and the Stones. I had more of a natural rhythm-and-blues swagger than a rock sensibility, probably because I'd heard more Stevie Wonder and Chaka Khan than Sex Pistols and Zeppelin. I fashioned all my vocal stylings for the band after Mariah, which meant the more riffs the better. The guys would go crazy and tell me to just sing the line the way it was written. And they were right. I was overdoing it, trying to show off all that I was capable of the second they let me sing. How many times did I nail kids on *American Idol* for doing just that? I was desperate and people could smell it. I wanted it so badly. I was so close to the music business at *Billboard,* and yet so far away from it.

Some of Gramma Trips' set list consisted of songs they had written themselves. I would try to make changes and offer suggestions, but I was quickly shot down. My job was to sing even when I wasn't always in love with their originals. It started to feel like piano lessons with Mrs. Kuo at age eight. I didn't want to play the things she wanted me to play. I wanted to pick my own songs and express my own ideas. Being in a band felt like walking on eggshells, never wanting to insult the person who wrote the song I really didn't want to sing. I, of course, also made the fatal error of getting involved with the bass player who had an on-again, off-again girlfriend. Word of Warning: Don't get involved with people you work with—it never quite ends up the way you wanted. I did this twice in my career, and both times I regretted it. This was my first experience with how alluring creativity can be. Put two people in a room together who don't find each other attractive but have a musical connection, and they will be headed in the wrong direction faster than a bullet train if they're not careful.

During this entire experience, I was working my full-time job at *Bill-*

board, which entailed taking a train from Scarsdale, where I had moved into my grandmother's house to be closer to my mother during her illness. I'd leave at around 7:45 A.M. in order to be at work by nine and then I would hop back on the train a little after 6 P.M. heading for Ossining, an hour outside of the city, for practice with the band. This was all in addition to taking care of my mom.

When I finally took stock of how taxing it all was and admitted to myself that I was just not feeling an emotional bond to the band's music, I came to the conclusion that I would be much better off as a solo artist. My newfound access to the center of the biz through *Billboard* gave me a bird's-eye view of what it took for a band to be signed. We needed a big following, which entailed touring, and I wasn't about to quit my job, leave my mother when she needed me most, and get into a van with four guys if I wasn't that committed to the music. So I left the band. I had to make a choice. Having cut that cord once, I was better prepared to do it again several more times in my career whenever the need arose. Sometimes you just have to leave your partners when it stops working for you or when you think you can go further without them. It's painful but you can't let guilt stop you, because it's your duty to go the distance in this lifetime and you don't owe anyone anything other than to always give 100 percent to them when you're with them, to be honest about it when it stops working, and to transition with respect and grace. Hopefully, the Gramma Trips guys think I did that.

Shortly after parting ways with them, I met a manager named Joe Lodi. He was referred to me by a DJ who had been working at one of the restaurants where I waitressed after college. While he was nowhere near being in the big time, he was kind and supportive and he gave me lots of encouragement when I needed it. I was insecure about my talent and unsure of what my next steps should be, and he was always there to help me sort it out.

Since I couldn't get anyone to give me a song, I made an impetuous decision to learn how to write my own material. Shit, what did I have to lose? I took a chance that ultimately paid off, but only after years of trying. Of course, I didn't know the first thing about writing songs, but it looked really easy from the outside. All I had to do was put together some melodies and rhyme a few words like "love" with "enough" and "heart" with "start." I had written a forty-page thesis in college, surely crafting a song less than a page in length was easier than that. And in an instant, I proclaimed myself a songwriter. What an idiot!

My first real writing sessions were in the Bronx at this musician/producer Dave Citron's house. I never had time for networking on my own. And I was definitely too busy to check out the club scene. So I relied on Joe to hook me up with the guys who were gaining traction.

The funny thing about Joe was he had this business installing ridiculous, off-the-hook custom-made car audio systems. Talk about pimping your ride. It was beyond rims, detailing, window tinting, and neon chassis lighting. This guy installed subwoofer boxes, tweeters, amps, full-blown competition systems, security alarms, and ironclad safes to stash cash, bling, and other valuables. Not that I ever knew what the hell he was talking about. But all this put him in big with urban record producers and artists. He heard lots of rumors about who were the latest up-and-coming talent, and soon enough he became a manager. That's how he found out about Dave. Apparently Dave had been playing keyboards for some of Joe's producer clients whose cars he was working on. Word was he was good, so Joe set up a songwriting session for us.

So we pulled up to Dave's pad very close to the highway. As I stepped out of the car I immediately heard dogs barking. Not just any dogs: these were Doberman pinschers and they were going nuts. I should have taken it as a sign to be careful about this move. As in "it could bite me in the ass." I ignored the barking and rang the doorbell anyway. I've always had more balls than brains.

The house smelled like incense, and Dave's exotic-dancer girlfriend didn't exactly give me a warm welcome. But I didn't care. I was there to do a job. I needed a hit. Dave began playing something on the keyboard and I started singing along. We wrote "Show Me," one of the worst pieces of crap I have ever heard. Everything about it sucked. Now, you have to know that

I mean no disrespect to Dave—it was me who tanked it. Basically the song was about getting the guy I liked at the time to show me his feelings—to admit that he liked me. Of course, this guy was not that into me, so the subject matter and the title ended up being plain stupid. Instead of owning my feelings and writing about how hurt and totally rejected *I* felt, I wrote about his inability to open up. He, of course, could open up just fine—he simply wasn't doing it with me! The song didn't work because I hadn't put any honesty into it. What did I know about how closed off from his feelings he was or wasn't? I should have been dealing with my own problems.

At the time, though, I thought I had penned a Grammy Award–winning tune. So many young writers and artists who come through my door think their early songs are undeniable hits. While they may have talent, the chances that they nailed a truly great song on the first, second, or even thirteenth try are slim to none. Most of them don't know themselves well enough yet to communicate their true emotions in a unique way that will move listeners. I certainly didn't. Before I could help others do that, I had to do it for me. I had to become my own therapist and shrink myself!

Reflections on Writing "Taking Chances" with Dave Stewart

All those chances I took early on—from making the decision to be a singer, to joining a band and later breaking up with that band, to going solo and writing my first song—were pivotal first steps. Ten years later I would get an opportunity to take another big chance with Dave Stewart. I had known Jimmy Iovine, the president of Interscope Records, for quite a while. He was one of my earliest supporters. He'd gone out on a limb for me before arranging introductions to various artists/producers signed to his label, but no one as big as the person he was about to introduce me to. Out of the blue he called to say that Dave Stewart from the Eurythmics had just thirty-six hours to work with me. Could I fly to London to meet with him? The prospect was both incredibly exciting and really odd at the same time. I mean, where did they come up with this crazy-ass time limit? Did that mean I had to stay up thirty-six hours straight or what? But really, who knew and who cared? I was gonna meet and work with a legend! Needless to say I was a huge fan.

I left the following day with my mission in hand. Dave Stewart and I were going to write for the Pussycat Dolls. I had no real idea who and what they were, but it sounded just fine to me. I landed at Heathrow in the UK and was driven straight to the studio to meet Dave and Nicole Scherzinger, the lead vocalist for the group. Within the first five minutes of our meeting, I felt like I had met my older brother from another mother. Dave was the funniest, sweetest, most eccentric and talented person I have met to date. Within twenty minutes he had literally handcuffed himself to me and we stayed that way until dinner with the then head of Universal in the UK. Our creative bond was instant, as the antics with the handcuffs indicated, and the music just poured out of us.

We had such a great chemistry that he invited me to work with him a month later in Los Angeles. Interscope Records sponsored my trip under the assumption that Dave and I would continue crafting songs for the Pussycat Dolls. Naturally I jumped at the chance and spent two weeks going over to his house on Kings Road in the Hollywood Hills and writing, drinking tea, and swimming in his pool. Dave was one of the only purists I have ever met. Up until that time I was a songwriter for hire, so I always started from a point of my truth and then adapted the lyrics to fit whomever I was working with or writing for. Not Dave. He didn't care about what we were supposed to be writing or who we were writing for. We were writing in the moment, and if it fit the Pussycat Dolls, great. If not, so be it.

So, we wrote about what we were feeling and let inspiration take us wherever it wanted to. On this occasion it took us nowhere near the PCD's album.

Our songs were bittersweet—about our loves, our sorrows, our joys, the world—and when it came time to play them for Jimmy Iovine, I had my checkbook out, ready to reimburse him for the full cost of the trip. Surprisingly, Jimmy loved the songs and said, "You guys should be a band."

Hell no, I thought. I'd been through that before and was really loving my job as a songwriter. I was not interested in anything to do with performing. But Dave's eyes lit up and it became his mission to convince me that we should do it. Every day he would take pictures of me and tell me I should dress more like the artist I was. He took me to Maxfield (a swanky designer shop on Melrose) and bought me a leather jacket for more money than I had ever spent on an entire outfit. He had some fancy hairdresser come to his house and give me highlights. He was trying to show me that I could be a performing artist if I wanted . . . but that was it, I didn't want to anymore. I had gone through years of rejection—from Ahmet Ertegun not taking me seriously as a teen, to no one believing in me enough to give me songs, to finally being dropped from a label early on in my career. I had tried long and hard to be an artist and I was over it. I had a great life. I could express myself without committing to any one genre, make a good living, and go home at night. But Dave wouldn't let up and his determination made me start to wonder if I should just give it another try.

One afternoon, I asked Dave to come to my house to write. I had just bought a place in Los Angeles; staying in hotel rooms and at friends' homes was starting to take a toll on me—and on them. I needed my own space. It just so happened that the day he came over the movers had arrived with all my furniture from New York.

Dave's temperament is the opposite of mine. He's calm, soothing, soft-spoken, and mild-mannered. So you can imagine how nervous he became when I started yelling at the movers to stop hitting the walls with my furniture. He does not like commotion, and in typically fabulous Dave Stewart style he went to his happy place. This particular happy place involved playing along with the wind chimes that were swaying on my porch. It was an easy enough distraction and soon he began to finger-pick the instrumental motif that would become the beginning of "Taking Chances," which, he humbly claims, were the exact notes the wind chimes were playing. Despite all that chaos and commotion, I was hooked.

Inspiration comes at strange times and places. It's like love. The more you want it and concentrate on getting it, the less likely you are to receive it. You have to let go and put your mind on something else and it will find you in its own time. I stopped my conversation with the movers in midsentence and sang, "Don't know much about your life." Then I went back to giving orders to the movers, only to stop once more a minute later to add the line "don't know much about your world." Clearly, they thought I was a nut job, but slowly the furniture, their paperwork, my irritation, and everything else in the world faded. Dave and I were having a conversation about being a band, weighing the pros and cons, and within thirty minutes the song reflecting that pivotal conversation was done.

From my perspective, "Taking Chances" was me finally saying yes to being in Dave's and my band, Platinum Weird, and saying yes to stepping out into the forefront once more. It took a lot of convincing by Dave to get me to a place where I would risk rejection again, but by that time the stakes weren't as great. I knew I would be okay if it didn't work out because I had actually started to value who I was and what I had accomplished. Nobody, even my most critical self, could take that away. While the band was eventually dropped, two great things, other than meeting Dave, came out of Platinum Weird. Céline Dion heard my rendition of "Taking Chances" and it became the title track for her tenth studio album, and Dave schooled me in making the transition from a behind-the-scenes songwriter to a front-and-center performer. It was that schooling that would help prepare me for the biggest chance I would ever take—live TV.

Four

MAMA'S SONG

"Mama you taught me to do the right things
so now you have to let your baby fly."

You don't know what you are made of until someone you love becomes terminally ill. I never thought I would see the day when I would have to change my mother's diapers and hold her in my arms like she was my child instead of me being hers. Or when I would have to tell her how proud of her I was because she held down a half cup of Cream of Wheat without violently throwing it up. Or frantically pick her up off the living-room floor, which we had converted into a bedroom because she was too weak to go up and down stairs. These are the moments that are life defining. The moments when you have to decide, do you run or do you stay and do the right thing? For me there was no choice. In my life, there is ONE thing I am most proud of and that is that I gave 100 percent of myself when it came to being there for my mother. Out of all the things I've done, that is hands down my biggest accomplishment and the shining star on my life's résumé.

It was supposed to be a normal hysterectomy performed by my mother's ob-gyn. So when my mother called me at college and said, "I have cancer," I was shocked. The last place you want to find out that your mom is sick is in your dorm room while you can hear people partying in the quad outside your window. The sound of carefree laughter juxtaposed with my utter speechlessness seemed so painfully ironic. The word "cancer" to me was equal to a death sentence. My mother assured me the doctors had gotten it in time. That's what they always say, but what they mean in more cases than not is that they got it in time to give you a little more time. I wanted to come home, but she insisted that I stay at school, so I did. I don't know how my mother really felt because she hid her emotions from me, but soon I would be witnessing firsthand what cancer does to those it strikes, and surprisingly enough, as horrid and undignified as it was, it brought my mother and me closer together.

Knowing you are facing death makes you look at your life in a completely different way. Early on in her illness, my mother made the decision to divorce my father, which was an interesting choice in that it meant she would not have a husband by her side when she was lying in a hospital bed and likely needing him most. My father came to visit often despite this. I never asked her why because I knew how unhappy she had been. My parents had stayed in their marriage much longer than they should have. I instinctively knew my mother wanted to prove to herself that she did have the strength to leave.

She went through three rounds of chemotherapy in six years. Whenever her remissions ended, the doctor would always say she only had months to live, but she continually beat the odds. She kept on going and lived each day to the best of her physical ability. Anticipating her death, I willingly put a hold on my own life. I stopped everything I was doing to spend as much time with her as I could. Doing anything other than being with her seemed pointless and I felt so incredibly sad to think she was sitting home alone with the knowledge that she was dying. Whether I was in the hospital crawled up in bed with her, helping her walk around the hallways while she was hooked up to an IV after surgery, or taking day trips to the water, enjoying seaside lunches, or cruising around Connecticut in our car when she was able to go home, she gave me the gift of the MOMENT.

I have always had trouble staying in the moment. For me it was always about what happened in the past or what I was going to do in the future. Nowadays cell phones, BlackBerries, beepers, instant messages, tweets, and even access to the Internet on planes keep us from enjoying our moments. Every day is filled with urgency, and before you know it, eighteen hours have evaporated and you realize that you never once felt the sun on your face or called a friend to just say hi. When I left *Idol*, I started to look around at my life again and notice all the beautiful things I had begun to take for granted as I got caught up in the pace and demands of the show. The view of the sun setting behind the mountains in my living room, pictures of my god-babies (Michael and Cami), and the way my husband smiles in the morning when he first sees me. I let these daily occurrences slip away as if nothing was as important as the press call, the photo shoot, or the free-gifting suite. Of course, none of these mean anything in the larger scheme of things and I thankfully started to remember the message I was given when my mom was sick. When you are dying, all you have is the moment, and since we are all "dying," this moment is all we are guaranteed. You can appreciate it, or you can miss it. It's your choice.

The moments my mother and I spent together were healing. I was my mother's primary caregiver. I took her to the doctors, administered her shots, doled out her pills, gave her enemas, and was in constant contact with her physicians. Another important Note to Reader: Always carry a pen and a notepad when you are talking to doctors. Write down everything they say and hold them to their word. Sick people are only numbers until they become potential lawsuits. We bought my mother a year and half by realizing that something was wrong with her doctors' protocol and by seeking a second opinion. I took her to the hospital when she was too sick to stay at home and waited in the lounge while her surgeries went on for as many as five hours. Every time a doctor came out I thought they were going to tell me, "I'm sorry—we did everything we could." And every one of those times, she kicked cancer in the ass . . . until there was nothing more they could do for her. That's when she was placed in my brother's and my hands.

At the end of my mother's life, I moved back into my grandmother's 2,500-square-foot home that had already been housing my mom, my brother John, and my ninety-three-year-old grandmother, who was grieving the impending loss of her only daughter. I became like a drill sergeant, fighting the enemy that was ovarian cancer. It was a skill that would serve me well later in life. By age twenty-six, I already understood a few things about the battle ahead of us.

1. It was going to get ugly. My mother's body was shutting down fast. She weighed less than one hundred pounds in the weeks before her death and my grandmother was saying the rosary every hour on the hour, begging for her daughter's life.

2. I was under the scrutiny of my mother's "friends," some of whom would come to visit her only to spend the time telling me what I wasn't doing right or trying to convince my mother of my ineptness. I had to not so gently remind them of their absence during the times when she was vomiting her guts out and falling to the floor. They were judging me, but where had they been?

3. Worst of all, I was losing my mother.

But what cancer did give us all was closure. Unlike a sudden death, with cancer you know it's coming and you can use the time to clear the air. I spoke with my mother at length about things in our relationship that had troubled me. I never thought she understood me and there were times I felt she didn't support my career choice or lifestyle. I listened to her side of the story, and I was lucky to have that honest dialogue with her before it was too late. I started to see that all of her opinions and desires for me came from a good place—a place of love.

I also saw another side of my brother. I stopped seeing him as this little boy with a lisp who I used to tease and started seeing him as a young, compassionate, loving, deep soul of a man. Many twenty-three-year-old kids in his position would have run and made excuses for why they couldn't be there. He didn't. He stayed by my mother's side through her darkest moments and he loved her until she couldn't feel that love anymore in her human body. Without him, I couldn't have endured her death. He was my mother's son—thoughtful, easygoing, and nurturing—and even to this day, when I look at him I know she is still with us.

My brother and I would trade shifts in the few days leading up to her passing. The night before she died, I took the graveyard shift. I could feel death in the room. It was heavy and solemn. My mother had not only lost her ability to speak, she would lie awake gasping for air and waving her hands. I sat next to her, pressing her palm to mine and telling her that I loved her while alternately filling out ad-sales paperwork for my job at *Billboard*. To this day I don't know why I was doing that. Why wasn't I screaming and crying and dying with her? I think it was an act of self-preservation to focus on something else, or I would have surely shot myself, or maybe even killed her so she didn't have to suffer any longer. My brother came down at around 6 A.M. to relieve me. I went upstairs to bed and shortly thereafter my uncle was waking me up to tell me that my mother was gone. My thoughts went immediately to my brother. "Where was John?" I cried. He had gone to get more diapers, and in that small window of time, she had let go.

As a kid, I would often ask my mom, "Who do you love more, me or Johnny?" Yes, even then I had narcissistic tendencies. And she would always reply, "I love you both equally." I understood my mother's choice not to die with either of her children present. It was her way of showing us that she really hadn't favored one over the other.

I body-bagged my mother. Yes, I actually watched them zip up the bag and carry her out of our house. From that moment on, nothing could touch me. I had lived through hell, and nothing else anyone said or did to me would ever come close to that moment. Not even thirteen years later, when people would publicly insinuate that I was getting the boot from *American Idol*. Oh please: that was nothing compared to a real life-and-death struggle. Thanks to my mom, on August 22, 1997, I was reborn as a fearless fighter—and was better prepared than ever to be a woman diving headfirst into the business of music.

In my lifetime I have been lucky to have had a biological mother and two other mother figures influence my life in profound ways. I have witnessed greatness in all of these women and have learned lessons from them that serve me every single day. My nanny Mary (the grandmother who loved music and played Debussy's "Clair de Lune" on the piano) gave me the unconditional love I hadn't always felt from my parents. I swear, she had a halo shining over her head and a very distinctive smell about her that for me was heavenly—I still get nostalgic for her whenever I catch a whiff of Pond's Cold Cream. I can't remember a time when I was sick as a kid that she wasn't there making me soup or rubbing my back. My brother received the same loving treatment. Nanny Mary understood the importance of family meals—something we never had much of at my house because my father was always working late. She would slave away in the kitchen for hours on hot summer days with no air-conditioning roasting a savory leg of lamb. She wanted us to be nourished by good food and good conversation. She knew that our time together was invaluable, and if my brother and I were not experiencing the closeness of family life daily, she made sure we did when we were with her.

Nanny Mary also had a wicked sweet tooth and would hide her treats because my grandfather was concerned that she was eating too much of what wasn't good for her. I could always find a bag of Pepperidge Farm's Milano cookies behind the curtains and other baked goods stashed in unlikely places. It was like a treasure hunt every time I went over to her house. She also had a habit of hiding her jewelry so I never knew where a pair of pearls would pop up in my quest to find a snack. She recognized my sweet tooth, too. When we would be together at the beach, she would go for walks with my mom and give my brother and me a wink, letting us know that while she was gone it would be okay for us to go in her bag and get money for a Fudgsicle, the treat my mother wouldn't buy for us at lunchtime.

My grandmother was a calming and grounding force for me growing up. She gave my brother and me stability. My grandparents had a wonderful relationship, so witnessing the way she cared for my grandfather showed me what marriage should be like. I followed their example when it came time to create my own home life. Nanny Mary was a consistently loving grandmother from the day my brother and I were born until the day she died. After my mother passed away, my brother and I took care of her until she had a stroke and was unable to move. We were lucky to have the opportunity to look after her the way she had looked after us all of those years.

My other mother was Marianne Dowling, the parent of my good friends Anne and Katherine Dowling. Marianne was a strong, opinionated, no-nonsense, financially independent woman. Most of the moms in Westchester County, New York, at that time were stay-at-home housewives who got their hair done and ran errands until their kids came home. Not Marianne. She was raising two kids on her own after divorcing their father and holding down a prestigious legal job at MONY. She was also one of the first women to make the Fordham University law review. What's more, she made the time to help raise a third kid (me) and to be our soccer coach on the weekends.

Forget Lynda Carter, Marianne was a true wonderwoman and a hero to me. There was so much friction between my parents in my own home that I spent as much time as I could at the Dowlings'. During those times, Marianne always encouraged me to study. Education was very important to her and her daughters. I am not sure I would have gone to Duke without her guidance, nor that I would have put school work first before my boy-crazy ways. I distinctly remember her displeasure when my first love, who had slept over one night after a terrible snowstorm, appeared in her kitchen the next morning disrespectfully wearing nothing but a towel and asking for shampoo. I'm sure she had visions of me being knocked up and pumping gas at the local Mobil station for the rest of my life. I could have easily gone down the wrong path had she not kept me on the straight and narrow. Marianne knew that education was vital to being a strong, independent woman who could make her own choices and avoid getting trapped in bad situations.

Unlike my own mother, who had never had a job and was hesitant to leave her marriage and the financial security it provided, Marianne was the one who made the rules in her house. She did not have to rely on a man for anything. Her autonomy opened my eyes to the realm of possibilities out there for a woman. I often think about how hard it must have been for my mother to know that I preferred to be at the Dowlings' home instead of my own. But in a strange way I think of her silence on the subject as further confirmation of my mother's strength. I think she knew that Marianne could teach me things she could not—things like how to be independent and take care of myself. Sensing that I wouldn't be content with just getting married, my mother knew that I needed other skills to achieve my goals, and she trusted Marianne to help guide me in those ways.

All three of these unique women shared and gave me one thing in common—a mother's love. That love was deep, unwavering, and guiding. I benefited immeasurably from having all of them in my life. Without their examples, I am positive I would not be who I am today. I hope someday soon to have my own child, and to impart the gifts these women gave to me to my son or daughter. I am sure that I will only further understand then how much these mothers really did for me.

Reflections on Writing "Mama's Song" with Carrie Underwood

Carrie Underwood's reputation preceded her as a powerhouse vocalist with a shy and quiet demeanor. I had never met her, but of course I knew of her music. Country was not what I was known for at the time, but you don't turn down a session with America's favorite sweetheart. She is one of *Idol*'s biggest success stories. The show came along, plucked her away from her small town, and put her smack-dab in the middle of Hollywood, granting her access she might never have had to the coveted music industry. And thank God it did as she is a triple threat—writer, performer, and beauty.

When she walked into the room, it was not a big grand celebrity entrance. Carrie is all business, and that is what has made her so successful. She is there to do a job and she will work hard until it gets done. She is appreciative of the opportunity that *Idol* has given her and she takes full advantage of it. I do not know one successful artist, or successful person for that matter, who does not work incredibly hard for their achievements. Success comes from putting in the time.

During our first two hours together, Carrie and I wrote "Undo It" (along with Marti Frederiksen and Luke Laird). I already had a loose chorus concept and some of the melody when I walked into the room. Carrie liked the bluesy quality of what I was singing, and before I knew it, we had completed the song. That was a good sign. Cowriting songs is like dating. You know within the first fifteen minutes if you'll be leaving after one drink or getting kicked out by the bartender at closing time. We were in for the long haul but we never could have guessed that we would be penning #1 and #2 songs at Country Radio in the five hours we were together that day.

I don't know how it happened or why, but shortly after writing

"Undo It," Carrie and I started talking about our love lives. She had only been dating the man who is now her husband for a short while and wasn't yet admitting that he was "the One," though she did confess that he had potential. Somewhere inside she must have known more than she was willing to say at that point because "Mama's Song" hinges on the realization that when we've found the right person, we all have the desire to let our mothers know that they shouldn't worry anymore—that we are happy and safe, and that she is not losing her child to anything or anyone. Her child is gaining greater love. My mother had always been concerned that I find the right man. I had and was glad I would be marrying him that summer. Although she wouldn't physically be there to see me walk down the aisle, this song in my mind was a message to my mother that I had found the life partner she had hoped for. I didn't play "Mama's Song" at my wedding, though. I was too worried it would get leaked. I hope Carrie played it at hers!

Both Carrie and I felt that the typical wedding song catered to the father and the tradition of him giving his daughter away. Pretty chauvinistic stuff. *What about the mothers?* we thought. The women who nursed us, changed us, taught us about the birds and the bees, picked us up from school, and taught us the difference between a tampon and a pad? This song was for them. And it was for people like me who had lost their mothers, too. In my case, I feel closer to my mother since her death than I felt during her life. Many daughters don't really appreciate their mothers until they are older and see just how these formidable women kept them alive and safe. The mere fact that so many of us are walking around relatively unscathed is a miracle, even if we are sporting a few scars you can't see.

Five

"You can run, you can hide,
but you can't escape . . ."

fter my mom died, the only thing I
felt like doing was running. I'm not
talking about a jog around the corner.
I mean sprinting until your heart feels
like it's going to pop out of your chest.
I ran from all the bad memories, the smell of vomit,
the death in her eyes, the incredible sadness, but
mostly I ran from the me I was at that time. I was
in search of the me I hadn't yet become and desperately wanted to meet her. Despite the earlier steps I
had taken toward self-reflection, I still did not have a
strong sense of my truth. In order to be a great songwriter, or artist of any kind, you have to be willing to

own the good, the bad, and the ugly in yourself. It wasn't until I embraced all those parts of me that I would be free to start writing good songs.

My early ones have never seen the light of day, thank God, because listening to them is like looking at a high school picture of yourself and thinking *How the hell could I ever have walked out of the house looking like that?"* But I value these songs anyway because they were my first attempts at boldly looking in the mirror, staring myself down and confronting the disconnect between who I was projecting myself to be and my reality. Obviously, I didn't have it together. The proof was my continuing addiction to food. I know I said that I was making strides in this area (I was a long way from those days in bed at college recovering from a binge), but my on-again, off-again relationship with excessive eating was proving to be like an abusive ex-lover, stalking me most when my defenses were down. And my defenses were definitely down again. I no longer wanted to hide the problem or myself. I wanted to see me for who I was and be committed to that self. But who was I? What did I have to say? What made me interesting? These questions had to be answered for me to make any kind of real and lasting changes in my life and in my music.

My search for me involved many early collaborators, including a wide range of people in the business such as Eddie Wohl, Dave Citron (whom I mentioned before), Rick Angelori, Gary Lue, Jon Wolfson, Derek Smit, Mitch Kaplan, Tony Moran, and Dan Wise, many of whom I met while I was still at *Billboard* working a day job. I was not a great player of any instrument at the time, so I relied on these guys for musical inspiration. If I could feel an emotion within their music and if it struck a chord in me (no pun intended), it meant that I had an experience to align with it. If the music was sad, it prompted me to talk about my mother or a troubled relationship I had been in. If it was happy, I stayed away from contributing, at least in the very beginning, because I wasn't emotionally there yet. In many ways music was my therapist. I had to continue searching within myself and shedding the pain before I could get to the joy.

With each song I dug deeper and found another layer that I didn't know was there. When I got down to the core, I was finally able to start turning my pain into a kind of currency, something I could really trade off of and express in my writing. But it took what felt like an eternity. The predecessors to my hits were songs like "I'm a Catholic," where the chorus described me as more of a depressed sinner than not. I should send the pope a copy of that one.

I was still working at *Billboard* during this quest to find me, which slowly evolved into a quest to find the perfect song to *showcase* me. I was almost ready for people to recognize Kara DioGuardi as an artist worthy of a record deal. My goal was to find four or five self-penned tunes that would represent my direction and the theme of my album. When I finally got to a place where I was proud of my work, I gave a tape (yes, back then we used tapes) to Larry Flick, the dance editor at *Billboard* magazine and the same person who introduced me to Paula Abdul.

Up until this point Larry and I had always had a contentious relationship. He called me "Runway" because I would march up and down the halls handing orders from my bosses to the staff members. I admit I had an air of arrogance about me but I was the head honcho's assistant and I needed people to take me seriously even though I was only twenty-two years old when I started that position. I wasn't exactly in love with Larry either. He played his four-on-the-floor techno music on blast and had a laugh that shook the building. I think his inability to be anyone but himself annoyed me because I wanted to be just like that.

Even though Larry and I had not gotten off to the greatest of starts, I respected him greatly. He championed artists and had a passion for music, so when it came time to get an industry opinion about my work, I went to him. He was a bit taken off guard, as my energy had changed from that of a mini Napoleon to a docile lamb. "Can I talk to you?" I asked.

"What's up?" he replied, almost as if he was confused at why I was being so nice.

I took him into the conference room (one of the big perks of being an assistant to the publisher was that I had the key and could use it at my disposal).

"I have a friend who thinks she's an artist and wants a record deal and I was wondering if you could do me a favor and listen to her," I lied.

He wasn't exactly thrilled at the prospect of helping me out, but he took the tape and said, "Okay, I'll let you know what I think."

For weeks I avoided going past his desk on the way to my own. I took the long way around the office to avoid him, which made me later than I usually was some mornings. Every time I heard his cacophonous laugh I shuddered inside, as it meant he could be headed over to me to deliver the brutal truth about my songs. Was I ready to hear that I'd better think about another career? I'd heard that line before. In my mind, everything hinged on Larry's opinion because he was so respected in his field. I was insecure about my potential, so if he didn't like what he had heard, it would have been like a road block signaling me to slow down, turn around, and come up with a new game plan. Hadn't I done that enough already?

It felt like I had waited years for his feedback and when he finally came over to my desk, he was smiling.

"This girl is really, really, really good."

"Oh my God," I squealed. Which seemed a bit much considering she was "just a friend."

"It's me," I blurted out. He looked at me like *Yeah, sure it is; now who is this chick really?*

"I swear it's me," I said. He looked puzzled. Here I was, a twenty-something-year-old, dressed in practical nine-to-five attire with bags under my eyes from squeezing in recording sessions before and after work and running across town to do demos on my lunch break. I looked haggard and unmarketable. Of course, he couldn't have known that I aspired to be a recording artist. Then he smiled. It took him a minute before he believed I was telling the truth, but I think he appreciated that I didn't put him in the awkward position of asking him to listen to "my" music. If he had hated it, how would he have broken the news to me? (Well, looking back, maybe gleefully.)

From that moment on, Larry and I were forever bonded. He saw me differently. Not as this uptight girl trying to impress her boss, but as an artist just trying to do her job so she could pay the bills and get out of there to do what she really loved—make music. Larry became my biggest champion to date, and without his early support, I don't know what would have happened to me. He listened, he critiqued and pushed me, but more important, he cared. He became my dear friend, and to this day is like a brother to me.

A few weeks later, Larry set me up on a meeting with a publisher at BMG named Clyde Lieberman. I knew enough about publishing to know that that's where the money was, but I had no idea what a publisher actually did. Little did I know I would own my own company years later. Publishers are like Match.com for writers. They continually pair you with other musicians and producers in the hopes that you'll have writing chemistry and make a hit together.

Clyde listened to my music with a judgmental ear. His first question to me was, "Do you want to be a star?" That threw me. I wanted a record deal but did I want to be a star? What exactly did that mean anyway? When he asked, I felt a bit queasy. Knowing what I know now, I see he was trying to determine if I was willing to have people look at me and judge me. Would I be able to capture people's attention and make them want to be me? Was I comfortable enough with myself to do all of that, and more important, did I have an artistic vision that would propel me into the public consciousness? Even though I couldn't bring myself to admit it, the answer back then to all these questions was no.

I believe there is a star in all of us, the part that is unique to each individual. My star at the time was like a lightbulb, flickering right before it dies. I still needed to do a lot of work on myself, identifying who I was, before my inner star would shine consistently and I'd be fearless about unleashing it.

When I played him my demo tape, he liked what he heard but felt I had a ways to go. The problem was that I was trying to be like every other artist out there. In my heart I wanted to be an R&B/pop singer, but there were no white girls doing that at that time. Christina Aguilera wasn't even a teenager then. So I abandoned the natural soul in my voice and tried my hand at pop/rock music, which was in fashion at the time with artists like Alanis Morrisette and Meredith Brooks. I sounded derivative, and it never occurred to me that real artists don't treat their music like Halloween costumes; one year a fairy princess and the next Little Chucky.

Clyde introduced me to published songwriters who were making money from their songs and I got on the so-called writing circuit. I went from session to session with different people who had varying strengths. Each challenged me in new ways and I learned from them all. In the beginning every one of us has inspiration—the force that moves us to say or sing something—but we haven't perfected our craft yet—the muscle memory that comes from doing something a million times. I had to hone my craft. I was a wild little colt who wanted to break out of the stable but had no idea yet how to use its legs.

Putting together the music that would finally convince someone to sign me as a recording artist took years. It entailed many cowrites with different people that resulted in hundreds of songs (none of which made me any real money, by the way) and more than ten thousand hours in the studio. Even then, the first song MCA signed me to record wasn't an original—it was a remake of "Walk on By." I was part of a male/female duo at the time under the uninspired name of Mad Doll. Although our contract was for a singles deal, we had been trying to convert it into an album deal by writing some originals. As far as I could tell, we were dropped from this label a short time later when the same executive who signed us couldn't convince Gregg Alexander, the lead singer of the New Radicals, to continue promoting his album and hit single "You Get What You Give," and was let go, putting all of this executive's other signings at risk. It seemed unfair to punish us just because the label was having issues with the executive whom we were working with. This was my first taste of record company politics. I was so disheartened by it all that when a producer named Tony Moran, who had heard the Mad Doll songs, asked me if he could cut one of them on an album for another artist, I began to seriously rethink my recording career. We agreed to let him have our song and it went on to become my first UK top-ten hit by Martine McCutcheon. I was a published songwriter. Not exactly what I set out to be, but I would take it for the time being. Who knew where it would lead me.

A few months later I hooked up with Paula and cowrote "Spinning Around." It was at that time that I decided to leave *Billboard*. I had always told myself that I would keep my job (at least on a part-time basis) until I was in a position to make a living from my music. The time had finally arrived to jump ship. It was do or die. I had to dedicate all my energy to music if I was really going to make something of myself, and if I wasn't going to be a recording artist right off the bat, then I guess I was going to try my hand at being a songwriter, which seemed ironic since no one thought my songs were good enough for me to sing.

Leaving *Billboard* incited a panic in me. I thought that having a few international hits would make it easier to be an in-demand songwriter. I was wrong. About a year after my exit, I began to second-guess myself, not sure if I had made the right decision. I could have had a great career at *Billboard*. When I left as a full-time employee I was making $75K a year in a sales position that could have really catapulted me up the ranks at the magazine. Maybe I had made the wrong decision. I decided to visit my best friend Suzie in San Francisco to help clear my head. Before I left for California, Clyde had given me the number of a manager to contact. The manager apparently had an up-and-coming producer client named Steve Morales he thought I could work with. When I phoned this manager, no one had gotten back to me. It was business as usual. I remember telling myself that if I didn't get a call by midnight that Sunday I was going to go home and beg for my *Billboard* job back. The manager called at 11:58 Sunday night and asked if I could be in L.A. by 1 P.M. the following day. I rented a car in San Francisco and left the next morning at 5 A.M. How's that for a close call?

I arrived in Los Angeles exhausted but ready to meet Steve. Could this be the musical partner I had been looking for? Someone who would bring the best out in me? His manager called and told me to meet them for lunch. I walked onto the rooftop of the Le Parc Suite Hotel and there he was. Five feet six inches tall, with gold crosses, diamond rings, baggy pants, and an

asthma pump, which he inhaled on while simultaneously smoking a Newport menthol. Was this a joke?

"Hey, Mama, I'm Steve," he said

First off, I ain't nobody's mama. Could this guy be for real?

"Hi, I'm Kara, nice to meet you."

"Sit down, relax, relax, you look so serious." He took a bite of his meal,
and while still chewing he asked, "You a writer?"

"Um, yes, I've written a couple of hits in the UK," I replied. Who the hell
did he think I was?

"No one cares about that," he said dismissively. "What about here?"

"Well, I've been—"

He interrupted me. "Okay, here's the deal. I'm the fucking best. I'm
gonna be the biggest. I got all kinds of shit going on and I need someone to
write to my tracks," he humbly said.

I thought to myself, *You better be because I just drove six hours to get here
and by the looks of you it was for nothing.*

"I'm gonna give you a track to work on. Meet me in the studio tomorrow
and we'll see what you come up with. Okay, Mama?" he said.

There was that mama shit again. Little did I know I would become like
his mama, taking control of all kinds of situations and cleaning up after
him, even loaning him the down payment for his house (he paid me back).

When I arrived in Los Angeles, one of the first things I did was call
Paula. She was out of town, but she offered her apartment if I wanted to
stay there. The gesture was a lifesaver, as I hadn't booked a hotel and wasn't
too familiar with the city yet. After meeting Steve, I went to her place and
immediately began writing to the track. The following day I went to meet
him at the studio. I walked in and there were four pretty hot girls from the
group Soluna sitting on a couch in the back all writing to the same track he
had given me to write to. I politely introduced myself as the writer who had
been hired to work on the track they were listening to. They seemed taken
aback, as if I had just told them I'd slept with all their boyfriends. They were
agitated and kept running in and out of the room.

Steve arrived late. I was soon to learn that one of his most annoying traits was running behind schedule—and not just by minutes, but by hours. He asked to hear the song and I sang it for him. He liked it and I felt good for the moment. But when I told him that it seemed like the girls thought they were going to be writing it, he said, "Don't worry about those bitches." Uh-oh, that didn't sit right with me. Had he just called those girls bitches? In my world that was no compliment. Then he instructed me to cut the vocals.

"Cut the vocals? You mean record each girl's part?"

"Yeah," he practically burped.

"Do the writers normally cut the vocals?" I asked.

"Of course," he answered as if I were being annoying.

I had no idea how to record a vocal group. I didn't know their voices or who should take what section. This was a disaster.

"Okay." I quickly asked each of them to sing and picked parts for them accordingly while Steve sat on the back couch flirting with one of them.

When I was done recording, he listened. My palms were sweating. The only recording I had ever supervised was of my own voice.

He laid his head on the console and shouted to the engineer, "Terrible. Turn those niggas down and turn Kara up."

No, he did not say that like THAT! (For the record, his continual use of the N-word in that session and for many years later made me physically ill. I despise that word and even though I now understand that Steve doesn't mean it in the historical way, for me and so many others, it will always have that negative connotation.)

The girls went nuts. They ran out of the room and hysterically called their manager. I was furious with him—for them and for me. Steve had totally set me up. He never told them that he had hired me to write for them and then he embarrassed us all. What the hell #$^&***.

I left the studio that night and got back to Paula's at around 3 A.M. The maid had taken some brownies out of the freezer and left them in the refrigerator for me. I had not eaten in hours. The stress of the whole day had made me lose my appetite, which never would have happened in the old days. I was supposed to return to the studio by 12 P.M. the next day, which I wasn't sure was a good idea in light of my first session with Steve. Before going to sleep, I shoved around six of these very small brownie bites in my mouth and hit the sack. When I woke up it was 11:30 A.M. Impossible, I am one of those people who does not need an alarm clock. I always wake up an hour before I am supposed to. As I raced out of bed, I fell flat on the floor. The room was spinning and I was shaking. I was convinced that I had a brain tumor. I stumbled down to the lobby and informed the attendant that I needed to go to the hospital. Next thing I knew, I was in the ambulance en route to Cedars-Sinai Medical Center. By this time I had lost my ability to speak and overheard the paramedic say, "This girl is as high as a kite." Was he talking about me? No way. I did not do drugs. How could this be? *Ohhhhh nooooo* . . . I suddenly realized. *THE BROWNIES.*

Yes, they were pot brownies that someone had ordered for a party and left at Paula's house unbeknownst to her. The maid, who was also clueless about the secret ingredient, had frozen them, and when she heard I was coming, she left them out for me. In all the years I have known Paula, I have never seen her drink or do drugs, so don't even think I am implying anything. You can only imagine how she felt when she found out! I was at the hospital for hours after that being rehydrated and infused with nutrients. When they released me, I had no money and could barely get myself into the cab that was called for me. For a moment I felt the kind of shame junkies must feel. Needless to say, I missed my session with Steve and ended up staying in bed for three days. I even had to explain to my family why I wouldn't be home for Father's Day. "Hi, Dad. I accidentally ingested some pot brownies and am too stoned to fly home." That was well received. As a side note, Paula's maid also ended up in the emergency room . . . after one small bite . . . and I had consumed six whole nuggets!

Being in Paula's guest bedroom for a few days nursing myself back to health reminded me of the last time I had been there. But that time it was Paula who was doing all the nursing. I had never heard about liposuction until I came to California, and was intrigued by it. Women on the West

Coast had that procedure as if it was an afternoon trip to the gym. They'd make an appointment for one and be back at work by seven. I was still struggling with those last few pounds and a small bit of the behavior that had caused them. So I looked in the *LA Weekly* and found a doctor who would perform the procedure for less than $5K.

Was I out of my mind? My choice of doctors was based on their own reviews—I didn't even have a referral! But I made a call to the doctor anyway and told Paula what I was going to do. Can you imagine having a houseguest who is supposed to be working on your record suddenly deciding to have surgery and turning you into her nurse? I promised that I would only need two days to get back on my feet, and since it was the weekend, I thought for sure that I'd be back to normal by Monday. She drove me to the doctor's office and picked me up. God bless her; she even cared for me while I was in bed recovering. Dammit, pain or no pain I was working two days later just as I said I would. I could barely walk or sit down, but I was there doing my job. Explaining my slow body movements to the vegan, holistic record producer we were working with was another story— it was like a scene from *Seinfeld*. But a deal was a deal.

Paula and I laughed uncontrollably about my impulsive liposuction, but on a serious note, for me, lipo was a huge step in my recovery. Spending thousands of dollars of my hard-earned money made me think twice about bingeing. I was obsessed with food but I was more into money, and there was no way I was going to waste a penny of it. Every fifty-cent Twinkie now had a $5,000 dollar price tag attached to it. I meant business about my 100 percent recovery from food addiction, and my willingness to part with that kind of cash at that point in my life was further proof that I did. I'd found a way to make my vanity and thriftiness work for me.

While liposuction was a major step in making sure I got my addiction under control, nothing worked better than doing what I love—music. I may still have been struggling with food in my twenties, but I was light-years away from the isolation I endured at college. Although eating all those brownies for dinner after the Soluna sessions felt like a momentary lapse into my old ways—a lapse I paid for dearly over the next few days as my "high" gradually faded—at least I was getting up with a purpose and I wanted something more than to self-destruct.

As it turned out, the girls from Soluna recut the song, it went on their album, and I kept in touch with Steve. Even though he was one of the most politically incorrect people I had ever met, I had to admit that he had a few things going for him. He could sell ice to an Eskimo; he was a talented beat maker and one of the funniest people I know. His methods for making music were unconventional but I was drawn to him—not in a sexual way, but because he was a drama queen and I was in search of something other than the loss of my mother to fuel my creativity. He let me do things he was supposed to be doing like recording an artist's vocal. He brought out the fearless in me and in this way I learned how to produce, speak up for myself, and go after what I really wanted. He also exposed me to urban music by locking me in his Mercedes and driving around for hours blasting Jay-Z, Tupac, and Brandy. My gut was telling me that my work with Steve was special and that there was a reason we were brought together. I was right. He put me on my first multi-platinum record, *Escape* by Enrique Iglesias. I am forever indebted to him for not locking me up in a crappy publishing deal (as many producers do when they put unknown writers on their records) and am thankful we met.

Reflections on Writing "Escape" with Enrique Inglesias

"Are you here for a lap dance?" Enrique jokingly asked when I entered the room.

"Ugh, no, I'm here to record your vocals," I replied. Although let's admit it, the man is "fine," so a lap dance would not have been torture.

Steve Morales had somehow gotten his hands on the Rolodex of a high-level industry executive, and when he came across Enrique's number the relentless pursuit began. He called him a million times until Enrique agreed to meet with him. Steve originally went into the studio to produce a song that Enrique had written, but he quickly saw an opportunity to write on the record, too. Naturally, he called me because I was his premier writing "nigga" (again, his term, not mine) at the time. I caught the first plane to Miami under the guise of helping him record Enrique's vocals, but I knew Steve would ghetto his way onto the record one way or another. And he did. I mean *we* did.

Together we wrote seven songs for *Escape* and the record sold 10 million copies. Translation: I could buy my own apartment in New York City and songwriting had finally become a big moneymaking occupation for me. We actually wrote "Escape" somewhere near the end of the record. I had been killing myself with eighteen-hour days, day after day. I had never worked with a "brand" voice before, someone who was already famous and had a recognizable sound. Nor had I heard any of Enrique's Spanish records. All I knew was that Enrique and I needed to write melodies and lyrics to the tracks Steve gave us and then I had to record the vocals as quickly and competently as I could. If I was scared shitless at any point, I had to ACT AS IF I wasn't (an important tool to use when trying to hide your fear and convince others that you can handle the task at hand). I had to carry myself as if I knew what the hell I was doing 24/7 or Enrique would get wind of it and possibly throw me out. This practice of flying by the seat of my pants served me well over time. The truth is, sometimes you just have to assume a role in life until you are able to fill it, and pretty soon it becomes as natural as breathing.

Enrique was a serious slave driver. He would get to the studio at around 5 P.M. and we'd work till 2 A.M. Then he'd want me back in the morning to compile the vocals into a lead vocal before he returned to hear it. The team consisted of all guys and me. They didn't need to shower or sleep but I did. I was a mess. I was so exhausted I even fell asleep during a haircut. When I woke up I had a a good six inches missing and was later questioned by Enrique about it. *"Oye, what did you do to your hair?" It was more like what was he doing to my life?*

On my only day off, I invited my best friend, Suzie, to meet me in South Beach, where I was staying. But as fate would have it, Enrique called me back to the studio that day.

"Oye." His famous opening line. "I have the track we need."

"Great, today's my day off," I snapped back.

"You have to come, I promise it's amazing."

"No," I firmly replied, even though what I really wanted to say was F-U.

"Yes, you must come now," he said.

"NO!" I shouted.

"Oye, get your ass in the cab and come," he demanded.

"Seriously, you're gonna make me work on my one day off?" I continued to protest.

"I promise it will be worth it."

He was right. Steve's brother, Diego, had been cleaning out his trunk and found the track which had originally been written for Soluna but they didn't like it. We came up with the melody line and somewhere in there he started saying "escape."

I went back to my hotel room and was really inspired by what we had done. Suzie was taking a shower and I couldn't get the song out of my head. I found a cocktail napkin (wish I had kept it) in the room and finished the lyrics to "Escape" right then and there. For me, it was about the relationship I was in at the time with someone who could not give me what I needed, but I wouldn't let it go and was trying to convince him that it could work. Sound familiar? The content was like my first song, "Show Me." I was still falling for the wrong guys, but in the meantime, I had gotten to know myself better and had learned how to really use my story to write songs. "Escape" was my first number one in the United States. I don't think it was a coincidence that the title of my first massive hit song was "Escape." I'd been trying to do that my whole life.

That same night was the only time I remember hanging out with Enrique during the whole record production. We went to a club and I marched right up to the front of the line and announced that I was with Enrique Iglesias and asked if they could let us in. Enrique was mortified but I didn't care. It was my one night off and I wanted to get in the club ASAP and dance, dance, dance with my best friend. I got a kick out of the big deal everyone made over having a celebrity in the club and must admit that I was happy to be on the outside looking in because the poor guy didn't get a minute to breathe. In fact, I was secretly laughing inside as I drank my white wine. The tables had been turned—now everyone was on *his* ass.

Six

PIECES OF ME

"I love how you can tell all the pieces,
the pieces, the pieces of me."

ince I don't have any biological children (though I do luckily have a fabulous stepdaughter named Elora), the closest I have ever come to having a baby, other than my dog Tikki, are my songs. Musical conception can happen anywhere. In bed, on the phone, or on the kitchen floor, which is where my collaboration with Katy Perry on "I Do Not Hook Up" took place (okay, so that doesn't sound exactly kosher), but most of my songs have been born in recording studios. For some reason, studios have become like church confessionals to me over the years. Maybe it's because most of them have no windows and they all tend to have paneled walls

that make you feel like you are isolated from the world and its judgment. I've walked into many of these soundproof rooms and have been able to hear my truth loud and clear. I've left pieces of me in all of them. I've also seen every facet of my personality emerge while writing songs. Some cowriters bring out the quiet in me, while others have awakened the crazy. Music is one of the only occupations where having multiple personalities doesn't result in an indeterminate stay in a mental institution. All those sides of you can actually result in great songs.

Intuiting what a profound experience writing a song can be, people have often asked me if it's hard for me to give my songs away. I've become accustomed to saying no, as it seems futile to get into a long diatribe about the pros and cons of it. But if I mentally take myself back to the first time I was asked if another artist could record my song, it still feels like what I imagine being branded with a molten-hot iron must feel like. Your brain processes this searing news as a message that you're not good enough to do your own song but someone else is.

As I mentioned before, I was signed to a singles deal by MCA Records back in the late nineties along with my bandmate Jon Wolfson (this was right before I met Paula). We had written several original songs we had hoped to record in addition to our single, a remake of "Walk on By." When that didn't happen, my friend and Martine McCutcheon's producer, Tony Moran, thought some of our songs were great and he suggested that Martine record them instead.

My first reaction was "Wait, you're going to give *my* songs to some *other* artist?" Actually, worse than a branding, it felt like I was cutting my arm off and auctioning it to the highest bidder, but what choice did I have? I was twenty-eight years old, I hadn't made a dime from any of my hard work in music, and was on and off a record label within what felt like all of five minutes. I got that this was a fickle business, but I had to figure out a way to make a career out of music. I was well on my way to recovery from my eating disorder and I knew that a lot of that had to do with being immersed in something I really loved. While I wasn't going to be a chart-topping performing artist anytime soon, writing for others (with the prospect of making income from that) would at least enable me to spend every day singing and creating, which was what I needed to be doing in order to stay healthy. Songwriting kept me in touch with my feelings, which kept me away from abusing food. So after weighing all the pros and cons, I agreed.

"I've Got You," which was the song recorded by Martine, was my first international success, but it was bittersweet. Not to say her rendition wasn't good, but I struggled to hear her pain, her joy, or some semblance of my own in it. That's when it really hit me that I had given my words and melodies to someone else. Singing was such an emotional release for me but sadly something about that emotion had gotten lost in her translation. Of course, I was asking a lot of her, as in my experience it's challenging for an artist to connect with a song they haven't written as strongly as the writer does.

While I was glad that the song did well, this first taste of giving a piece of me away was especially difficult because I had never met Martine. I had never had a chance to tell her what the song meant to me, why I had picked that lyric instead of another, or who it was about. I wondered, *Weren't those details important to anyone else but me?* I never admitted it to myself, but it bothered me that I gave what could have been *my* single to someone else. While I made my first giant leap into the business of music with that song, the truth is it hurt like hell.

I'd like to say it became easier after that to write and give my songs away, but it didn't. Initially, I tricked myself into believing that it was for the best and that at least the music wasn't going to sit in my closet, where my grand-kids would discover it one day and say, "Grandma, I didn't know you could sing." The checks helped lessen the blow of hearing another artist's rendition of my song, too. The more money I made, the quieter that ambivalent voice inside my head became, and the less intense the stabs to my heart were. Truth be told, by that point I began wanting financial security a little more than maybe I wanted to be a recording artist—and I wanted it without having to get a "real job." My work as a songwriter gave me a certain degree of insurance.

But even as I embraced songwriting more, there were always these little hiccups. Hearing someone else's interpretation of your song can be intense but hearing someone copy what you did on the demo word for word and breath for breath is worse. I know imitation is the highest form of flattery, but that was really unsettling, especially when your vocals are left in the final recording for support. But I still sang my heart out on those demos because I always thought that my task when writing was twofold: one, to write the song from an honest place, and two, to sing it as if I were the artist. I would emote so the listener could feel what I was going through. I had a knack for doing that. I could layer any sentiment I was feeling into my voice, making the artist more apt to want my songs, because they were reacting to my experience. Not only was I giving them my words and melodies, but I was also providing a vocal and emotional template for them to follow.

You can only imagine how confused I was. I'd think, *If I wrote the song, nailed it on the demo, and showed the performing artists exactly how to do it, too, why wasn't I the performing artist?* What I realize now, of course, is that while I had command of the songs' emotional content and even had the vocal goods, I never had a clear overall vision for the direction of my career as a performing artist or even a commitment to a single genre of music. Stylistically I was all over the map. I had never branded myself. My songs logically had a better shot in the hands of those artists who had or, at the very least, in the hands of those with solid platforms. Oddly enough, it was the diversity of my skills, including the ability to use my voice to communicate emotion that made me such a successful songwriter.

In fact, many of the producers I worked with would take my vocal map and adhere to every nuance without giving me any credit for my role beyond songwriting. They saw it as the songwriter's job to sing the demo. What they didn't acknowledge was that I did it better than most others because my interpretations were coming from a truly artistic place. When my combined skills began to help me rack up hits, I started fighting with the producers to give me vocal production credit, arguing that I was helping them do their job better by laying out the vocal arrangements and melodic inversions so effectively. It was frustrating because these guys were making $50K per production just to follow my lead. It was a real battle. They never saw it the way I did and it ended a lot of creative relationships as I resisted being taken advantage of. Most nights, I would leave the studio exhausted by the intense emotions I had poured out in the songs or transferred to others while vocal coaching. As I became more and more successful, I resented not getting the credit I deserved. I kept my mouth shut early on in my career because I wanted the work. But a lot of me was on those records—my hurt, my love, my weakness, my strength, my talent. At times it felt like I was being hooked up to an IV for someone else's benefit.

With my increased success, I began waging battles I knew I could win, whether it be for my production or songwriting abilities. Here's a quick story about one such fight to be paid what I deserved. Enrique Iglesias is a notorious prankster. We always have fun in the studio together. But when we cowrote "Somebody's Me," the jokes went a little too far. Now, you have to understand that I am incredibly indebted to Enrique. He was the first big artist to believe in me, but I was working on my third album with him by then and my career had really taken off. I was not willing to be as generous in terms of my publishing compensation as I had been in the past and his "but I took you on my plane" reasoning wasn't gonna sway me. By then, I could get my own private plane ride. Embroiled in a dispute over payment, I was listed on the album as Kaka DioGuardi. I thought the misspelling was odd, as I had been listed on many albums for that same label before. Surely someone would have noticed and corrected the spelling. I doubted it was a typo even more when a woman in my office who spoke fluent Spanish told me that *kaka* meant "shit." Great—*kaka* means "shit" and *DioGuardi* means "God Protects," so "Shit God Protects" is the literal translation. My dad *loved* that one, and I was just as pissed. Enrique claimed he had nothing to do with it, but since I had already been subjected to his antics before, I still didn't believe him.

Back when he was promoting the *Escape* album, he asked if I wanted to do backgrounds for his appearance at the Z100 Jingle Ball at Madison

Square Garden. For a native New Yorker, it didn't get much better than the Garden. I would be with two other backup singers, so I wouldn't be alone. I'd written most of the parts and thought it would be an amazing experience. Well, about forty seconds into the song, the background singers dropped their jackets, revealing these ridiculously skimpy outfits, and started doing an elaborate dance routine. I was standing there dying of embarrassment. I ran off the stage and the guards ended up quarantining me, thinking I was a crazed fan. I told them I had written the song and they were like, "Sure, sweetie." When Enrique got offstage I told him to tell the guards who I was. He said he'd never seen me before and laughed.

He eventually vouched for me but you could see why, years later, when I got a chance to exact some lighthearted revenge for the "Kaka" miscredit, I did. When he had to seek my permission to use "Somebody's Me" on *Dancing with the Stars*, I made him sweat it out. His people called several times wanting to know if it was a go, since the song was his next worldwide single and the show was a big promotional vehicle for it and his subsequent album. He would have been screwed if I had said no. I withheld my approval right up until minutes before the show, when he called me, and I finally gave him the okay. It's probably not cool that I messed with him that way, but it does speak to the issue of how when you are giving a part of yourself in a song, payback in the form of proper credit (like your name being spelled correctly) and money are important. Any other kind of payback is a bitch.

To this day, I fight for compensation and credit, even after having songs on 159 million records. The difference is that now when I call people out on their shitty behavior, they listen and they correct it. The tides shift. You've just got to stay in the water long enough for that to happen. Anger can be a great motivator, and I don't mean the kind that's so toxic it cripples you emotionally and physically. I mean a rage that says, "I know I am better than this and someday I will get where I am going if I just keep moving. If I don't let anybody or anything stop me along the way." Inertia is the tendency of objects in motion to stay in motion and objects at rest to stay at rest. A young talented artist understood this concept and once told me, "Keep it movin'."

And I did. I moved so fast that you couldn't keep track of me. I thought that if I was going to get less than I should, I had better work harder. Having smaller pieces on a greater number of records would collectively add up to what I deserved. More sessions meant a better chance of getting my songs on records, too. Before I knew it, I was on *everyone's* albums—from Britney Spears's to Christina Aguilera's. People were talking me up around town and it felt great.

Even though part of my aim by that time was to reap the financial rewards of songwriting, my process has always remained pure. I don't keep a lyric book or titles or have any preconceived notion of what I want to write. I only rely on those things in a worst-case scenario, when I'm working on music for a movie or a TV scene and something specific needs to be conveyed. Mostly, I walk into a room and *feel*.

Good songs come from a place of truthfulness. The process of songwriting led me to mine. With each song I felt stronger and got to know myself more. If I didn't know what I was feeling when I walked into a writing session, you could be sure that I'd have a real handle on it by the end of the day. Songwriting was my therapy, it was my religion, and it made me get to know myself in a way that I hadn't known myself before. Sometimes I had to tell my brain to shut up because my heart meant business. Your mind can trick you into believing anything. It reacts at times inappropriately to fear, insecurity, and doubt, but your soul is more apt to point you in the direction of you. The better I became at discerning what I really felt, the easier it was to help others do the same. When I cowrote "Sober" with Pink, I could easily access the pain of addiction because of my own issues with it. We were on common ground, so tapping into that place was easy. When she sang the song, she needed no template. Every note in it was laced with feeling because she had actually had the experience.

There were other times in my career when I worked with artists who didn't have much to say, so I lent or gave them my story and feelings. I offered it to them cautiously at the beginning, but far more freely as I got older. I recognized that it wasn't their fault they were less prepared for these writing sessions. Many of them were young and did not have a wealth of experience to draw from. I realized it was my job to find our common denominator—the place where we both felt the same way at one point or another in our lives—so that I could help them communicate those feelings in their music. It was easier for me to throw my life out there and see what sparked something in them.

We all know what it's like to give of ourselves. Sometimes we do it with reckless abandon, failing to acknowledge the consequences or to take a hard look at why we are doing it. There were times I felt I had given myself away too freely in these exchanges. Had I sold my soul as an entry fee into music? What I didn't realize back then was that it was my ability to get a grip on my pieces that made me such an asset as a songwriter. Once I embraced that, it no longer felt like I was giving anything away—I was using all of my hurt, pain, love, and loss to heal myself and others. My pieces were what I had to offer in a writing environment, in addition to my vocal interpretations. They were what was unique about me, what I could throw out there as inspiration for others to react to. What had once caused me to binge eat was now gaining me access into rooms with some of the biggest superstars. These pieces were my currency and without sharing them I am not sure I would have had the prolific career I've had.

At the end of the day, I can honestly say that I did what I had to do to stay in music and stay healthy; I took a much needed in-depth look at myself and my feelings so that I could bring them to the surface and release them, something I would never have been able to do on my own. I'm thankful to ALL of the artists I've worked with for enabling me to make a living from what I love to do and for being a part of my growth. Those parts of me may not have existed on my own album, but they ultimately found their way into millions of people's homes and hearts through other artists. I get to visit the best results of these pieces frequently in the form of a note from a fan whose life has been touched by a song, an artist's thank-you, or even during an *Idol* audition when someone's rendition of a song I cowrote resulted in a yellow ticket to Hollywood. Gregg Alexander of the New Radicals was right: you only get what you give. Realizing that I no longer needed to hold on to the pieces anymore, I sold my entire catalog to Bug Music, an independent publishing company. And I have never once regretted it. My advice: take time to get to know your pieces. You may come to some painful realizations in doing so, but you will also discover what is unique about you . . . and being unique can be valuable.

Reflections on Writing "Pieces of Me" with Ashlee Simpson

After "Escape" became a big hit in 2002, I was more in demand as a writer and started to meet the many movers and shakers in the industry. I was scheduled to work with Matthew Gerard (one of the cowriters on Kelly Clarkson's massive hit "Breakway") when I got a call from John Shanks (a prominent producer in the business who I had recently cowritten "One Heart" for Céline Dion and "Come Clean" for Hilary Duff with).

"You need to come to the studio right now," he said.

His studio was in West Hollywood, and I was already within minutes of pulling into Matthew's place in Santa Monica, at least thirty minutes away.

"I can't, I have another session," I said. That never flew with John. He was a bit of a jealous writing partner.

"Well, I would cancel it if I were you and come here," he replied.

Now, canceling on a writing session the minute it's supposed to start is like calling a date who's already at the restaurant having his first drink and saying you can't make it. It's rude and usually not very well received.

But my gut was saying, *Turn that car around.* I hated myself for doing it, but I canceled and went to Henson studio in Hollywood instead because I knew something big was about to happen. Note: One of the golden rules for success is to listen to your gut even when it means having to do something that's hard to do.

When I entered the studio, there were lights and wires everywhere. I tripped and said, "What the eff is going on here?"

John proudly replied, "We're writing for Ashlee Simpson."

"Who the hell is Ashlee Simpson? " I said.

"She's Jessica Simpson's sister."

Jessica was a big artist at that time whom I had written for, but I didn't know she had a sister who could sing.

"You got me to cancel my writing session for this?" I said.

"Yes, I did, and you'll thank me later."

John was right. He and Ashlee had come up with the title "Pieces of Me" already and the track was finished, too. He played the music for me and within the hour the rest was written.

Later that evening I was introduced to Ashlee. Meeting her was like meeting the girl I'd wanted to be in high school. Believe me, every kid thought so until that ill-fated *Saturday Night Live* performance. (Which wasn't her fault. She should never have gone on a prestigious live TV show like *SNL* with laryngitis, and the kid drummer should never have been in charge of triggering the track. She was ill advised and got the short end of the stick.)

Ashlee had this jet-black hair, a mischievous smile, and an uninhibited nature. Back then she was free. Free in the sense that she wasn't trying to look or be like her sister, Jessica. She knew she had a different appeal, so she embraced her rebel side. Did she know I had also been a rebel in high school? That one time my friends and I drove down the Hutchinson River Parkway with the convertible top down wearing only our bras? Of course, there was tissue paper everywhere.

I think we are drawn to different people at different times in our lives and there is always a lesson in our meeting. I felt incredibly creative around Ashlee because I was allowed to be the seventeen-year-old girl I had always wanted to be. I was able to live out my fantasy of teenage badassness and say unrepressed, un-Catholic things like "you make me wanna la la" which was about doing "it" in unexpected places. Who we choose to surround ourselves with can make or break our success. Some artists and producers simply move and melodies/ lyrics come pouring out of me, while with others, it's like pulling teeth. I wish I had spent less time beating myself up when it didn't work and more time seeking out those relationships that did work.

With Ashlee, songs came to me quickly and ferociously. Like they had been waiting for years to flow out of me. I buried my teen angst, broken heart, and longing for love in her first album. She was the perfect person to carry these pieces into the world. She was on a hit MTV show, and she was young and fearless. She was an embodiment of everything I wasn't as a teenager. I was happy a piece of me was on her record. Since I was there when the cameras were rolling I thought, *Surely I will be acknowledged for my contributions.* After all, "Pieces of Me" was about a long-distance relationship I had been in where literally Monday I was "waiting," the next day "fading," and the day after that I "couldn't sleep."

I was so excited for the premiere of *The Ashlee Simpson Show* that I told all my friends and family to watch it. I was going to get my recognition and show everyone that I really was a successful songwriter. Seeing me in action in the studio would provide undeniable proof that a mere name on an album sleeve could not. And then I saw it: my knee. Except for that least favorite body part of mine, they had completely cut me out of the segment on creating "Pieces of Me." It showed Ashlee talking about how she had come up with the song and John playing while she sang along. I was furious and embarrassed all at once and ended up screaming at the TV screen in front of another artist who was watching with me. "That's it, I'm calling my lawyer," I said, feeling really empowered by the idea. By the way, whenever you're really angry about something, wait a good twenty-four hours before you do anything about it. Or write your thoughts down in a letter and send it to yourself. Whatever you do, don't make decisions when you're in a highly emotional state or when you're tired. Trust me; you won't get the outcome you want.

I hastily instructed my lawyer to take whatever action against MTV that he could, tell Ashlee's manager, Joe Simpson, to go fuck himself, and contest my split on the song. I felt violated and robbed. Not a good combination. But I was not in a position of power on this one. In the end, I did not take any action. Yes, I had been omitted from the show but I was credited on the album, accepted what had happened, and moved on.

Unfortunately, I would feel like I got less than I deserved a lot in my career. I was learning that there was injustice everywhere. People will screw you out of money and credit on big records, just as easily as they do on small ones and every other kind in between. My instincts were always to fight the good fight. To blow the whistle on everyone. To take on City Hall. Blah blah blah.

But when reason finally prevailed, I had to ask myself: if I ratted out the perpetrators of credit crimes, or the people using my voice, or messing with me on splits of songs, where would that get me? Would it really enable me to put a roof over my head and continue to hone my craft as a songwriter? Or would it close every door on me from that point forward? I knew then that I just had to suck it up for the time being and embrace the bigger picture. I got to make a living from what I loved to do. I had much more left to say, much more to accomplish, and I had talent on my side, too. None of these motherfuckers were going to stop me. So I told the pieces that were left inside me to shut the fuck up and do their job . . . and eventually I got my due.

Seven ·

I DO NOT HOOK UP

"Oh no, I do not hook up, I go slow,

so if you want me I don't come cheap,

Keep your thing in your pants, your heart on your sleeve."

nyone who knows me knows I L-O-V-E men. I admire the way they're able to convey in one sentence what it takes me four to say. I think it's hilarious when they bust on each other and try to show who's got the bigger d***. I even get a kick out of how predictable they can be when a hot girl walks by. In my lifetime I have laughed harder with men than I do with most women and would pay money to be a guy for one day just so I could go to Vegas and experience my own version of the *The Hangover*. Men rock!

However my encounters with men in the music business have varied greatly. Some of them were supportive and nurturing when I needed it most, while others downright terror-ized me. Throughout it all, though, one thing was for certain: I would never use my sexuality to get a record deal or a song on an album. I had way too much respect for myself and knew that if I were to get the golden ring, it had better be because I earned it and not because I was good on my back. When you are not in a power position, sex is not your play. The goal is to be a self-made, independent woman following your dreams, not to be known as some guy's girlfriend. You want to be their colleague, or better yet, their BOSS.

Being raised Catholic is a real head trip when it comes to men. They are like cookies in a cookie jar to a compulsive eater. You see them every day in the kitchen, but don't you dare eat them all. You'll go straight to hell . . . or worse, fat camp! On top of being raised Catholic, I was at a distinct disadvantage for meeting guys at my then all girls' high school. The only men I ever saw there were the headmaster, Mr. Butts (my unnaturally thin English teacher, who was sadly named for a body part he didn't have enough fat to fill), and the janitor (who, by sophomore year, was actually starting to look pretty hot to all of us horny teens).

As a result, I guess you could say I was both uncomfortable around and fascinated by men. Somehow knowing the consequences of being pregnant as a teen (death at the stake) was the only preventative measure I needed. That, and the fact that my Italian-Albanian-Catholic father was a United States congressman who was staunchly anti-choice/pro-life. Let's just say I never wanted him to open the local paper to a headline that read "Daughter of Anti-Abortion Congressman Seen Leaving Clinic" because I knew what would happen to me if he did. Funny how you spend your whole youth trying *not* to get knocked up, and then, when you want to be, it doesn't happen. This was definitely true in my life, as I am on my fourth round of in vitro (three of them failed during Season 9 of *American Idol*).

My fear of pregnancy was further compounded by an unfortunate event that has affected my sexuality to this day. One of my mother's close friends had a son who was significantly older than me. As kids, we would always play hide-and-seek. But by the time I was eleven and he was in his late teens, it became a game of hide, seek, and touch. On one particular day, he took me into the back shed of his house and put his hands all over my breasts and vagina. I remember freezing and not knowing what to do. I had all these inchoate emotions including fear, shame, and confusion. He was, after all, "family." This happened a few more times, and while it was violation enough, the real hurt occurred when I told my mother and she chose not to confront the situation, but rather ignore it like it never happened. I can't tell you how much this cut me to the core. I had to continue to see him at family gatherings and I even sang at his father's funeral. The seed of distrust for men was planted then, and only grew from there. It was heartbreaking to know that my own mother could betray me this way. In time, I found the strength to forgive her. One could rationalize her actions away: she was a product of her time; there were no Oprahs then to help women handle such complex issues; she always had a fear of confrontation and this subject was not an easy one to tackle. There are even some people who suggest that parents don't show their concerns under these kinds of circumstances because they don't want to make their child feel more damaged by the experience. But, I really don't believe in making excuses. Nor do I believe in dwelling on bad things. There's no true healing in that. Instead I just put these memories someplace in my mind where they won't mix much with the fonder ones of my mother. We all sometimes use a loaded phrase when we talk about our parents. In my mother's case the phrase implies that "yes, she disappointed and hurt me at times, but she also raised me, loved me, and evolved into a better person each day, right up to the bitter end." So I know you'll understand what I mean when I say, "She did the best she could. Both of my parents did."

If you think about these events and how they affected me just for a second, you'd see how ironic it is that I ended up in the line of work that I did. To say that the behind-the-scenes music business is mostly comprised of men is like saying China is mostly inhabited by Asians. Being surrounded by mostly men in my industry was inevitable. Sometimes they were extremely attractive, as in the case of Enrique Iglesias. I have to admit that there were times when Enrique leaned over the console next to me and I wanted to faint. He was very good-looking, always tan and buff. There was also his accent. He hated it and was so self-conscious about it. "*Oye*, can you hear the accent?" he'd ask. "Yes you can, and it's soooooo . . . I mean no, of course you can't," I'd reply. Accent or not, my only goal was to get songs that I had written onto his record. And to his credit Enrique never once hit on me. A smart artist knows that when you are working with someone talented it is better to get a hit song from that person than it is to get a potentially bad hookup that would interfere with your creative chemistry.

A woman on the creative side of the music business is rare. A somewhat attractive one is almost unheard of. If given the choice between working with a gross, smelly dude or a female, the male artist, writer, or industry executive will invariably chose the latter. I may have worked my unique position as a selling point on occasion, but let's be clear, I DO NOT (DID NOT) SLEEP WITH ANYONE TO ADVANCE MY CAREER, and it should be the number one rule we are taught as young women.

One of the first meetings I ever had with a male record executive during the early days when I was promoting myself as an artist to prospective labels turned out to be the epitome of a music industry cliché. I sat in the lobby of one of the major record companies, with a pit in my stomach and a tape in my hand, for what seemed like hours until the temp working the front desk said, "Carla Delaguardia."

That had to be me. "Yes," I said.

"Rick will be out to see you shortly," she replied.

After another thirty minutes or so, Rick (I've changed his name for the purposes of this book) emerged to greet me. He was surprisingly pleasant and well mannered for someone who had just kept me waiting a ridiculously long time. (Note to Reader: I never keep people waiting more than fifteen minutes. It's rude and uncool. Our time is important no matter who we are or what we have done.)

After I followed Rick into his office, he closed the door. That was the first clue that this story was not going to end well. Note to Female Readers: Doors should always remain open for first meetings with a man you don't know. We listened to my music for a while and he seemed to genuinely enjoy it. But then again, everything seems genuine when you want approval. He mentioned a handful of popular producers at the time who he thought might be good collaborators for me. I was eager to meet any and all of them. He promised to call me after he had had some more time to sit with the music and I left the office walking on cloud nine. I even treated myself to a big serving of a not-so-low-calorie frozen dairy treat. I didn't worry for a second about the postindulgence weight gain, as I was convinced I'd work it off on the new treadmill I was buying once I got my big fat advance check from my new record deal with Atlantic Records.

My only problem was that this big fat check was never coming. What came instead was a phone call from Rick that really shouldn't have surprised me as I think back on it now. At that exact moment I was making dinner for my boyfriend. While I loved food, cooking was not one of my strong suits, but I tried to be as domestic as I could be (which usually meant one home-cooked meal per month). I'm not 100 percent sure, but it might have even been a celebration dinner, since I'd gushingly told my beau all about my impending artist contract. Anyway, the call went something like this:

"Hey Rick, how are you?" I asked.

"Good, good. I've been thinking about our meeting and you," he replied.

"That's great, because so have I, and I am really excited to meet some of those people you mentioned."

Then he dropped it, but not in the eternal words of Snoop, because "it wasn't hot."

"I had a dream about you last night," he said.

No, this is NOT happening, I thought. But it *was* happening. He began to talk dirty to me on the phone for the next few minutes while my boyfriend stared at me hopefully, thinking the news was positive and that I was already scheduling my first music video shoot. Rick went on and on about how he wanted to sleep with me and how he was wondering if I did threesomes. After a lot of "no's" and "I've got to go's," I hung up the phone and never heard from him again.

I knew right then and there that I was no longer in high school, where, if a guy tried something with you at a school mixer, he was likely to get tapped on the shoulder and asked to leave.

No, the only person who was going to save me was me. I needed to get me some armor, and the quickest thing I could think of came in four-letter words. "Fuck," "Shit," "Bitch" (oops, that's five). If I had the mouth of a truck driver, maybe these guys would just concentrate on my talent and not my tits (which, truth be told, were less than stellar by California standards).

Sadly, I would continue to face these types of situations for years to come and it would kill me inside every time. I was never flattered by the attention. In fact, I thought to myself, *I don't think I'm hot, and they're still hitting on me, so my music must really suck.* It can really mess with your head.

But it was the physical advances that did the most damage to my psyche. Back in 2000, Steve Morales and I were working out of Emilio Estefan's studio and a fairly well-known producer signed to Emilio had seemingly taken an interest in my songwriting. He asked if I wanted to have dinner with him one evening. I was alone in Miami for months and really didn't know anyone other than Steve, whose idea of a good time back then was dinner at Denny's and a lap dance at the local strip bar, so naturally I accepted the invitation. I was looking for a friend, someone I could talk shop with. Someone who might even give me some career advice. I didn't get that. Instead, within just a few hours, he was on top of me, pumping, sweating, and speaking to me in Spanish, not a word of which I could understand. The thing about date rape is that you don't know it's happening to you until it's too late. I mean, you know the person who is doing it to you, you chose to be in their company, and maybe even agreed to hang out and talk more after dinner, but does that mean you consented to engage sexually? I did *not*. I became frozen just like that first time someone had touched me inappropriately as a kid. It was as if my body was there, but my mind was somewhere else. All I could do was think of his daughter and wonder how someone with such a nice kid could be such a monster. I was scared, too, because I did not know him well enough to know whether he would become violent. On top of that, I was doing business with the music company he was affiliated with. I was in the ugliest of predicaments. I said no repeatedly, but if I hit him in the face or kneed him in the balls to make that point, I would have been out on my ass come Monday. He would have made up some story about me to his powerful boss that could have jeopardized my entire future. And I was getting closer and closer to breaking into the U.S. music market.

When he finally left my apartment, I crawled under my bedcovers and stayed there all night and the next day in a state of complete shock. I couldn't believe what had happened. He had been so friendly to me at the studio. I had talked openly to him about my life. I thought we were friends, or on our way to being so. There wasn't a single warning sign that he was a dirtbag. He was so smooth that I felt ashamed of being taken on every level. I kept going over and over the events of night in my mind. Did I ask for it? Was I dressed inappropriately? Did I say something that could have been misunderstood? When you have to ask yourself these questions, chances are you have been taken advantage of. It's sad that women have to even go there. NO means NO, no matter what you are wearing and what you might have said. You don't owe a man anything at the end of the night no matter what he's paid for. From then on I resolved to always split the bill.

A few nights later, when I was feeling stronger, Steve and I went out to a dance club. I desperately needed to tell someone about my traumatic experience. I don't know why I chose to confide in Steve, but I guess in a strange way he was my family for a short time. As fate would have it, we ran into my assailant at the club. I spotted him and immediately walked up to him and said, "I know what you did to me." He laughed and said I had wanted it. But in that one moment of confrontation I got my power back. I acknowledged to him and to myself that he had violated me. Witnessing this from across the room, Steve came over and threatened to kick this guy's ass, which was a bold move considering it could have cost Steve work. But Steve backed me anyway, and it felt good to know he cared. From that point on, Steve had my loyalty and trust. I knew I was under his protection. There I was, a Duke graduate, learning a thing or two about the "gangsta" way of life. Kill or be killed, stand up for yourself or die, and never let anyone take from you what's yours and yours only to give.

I would run into a similar situation a few years later with a well-known, hugely successful international artist. After that unfortunate event in Miami, whenever I worked with men I was even more committed to making sure I concentrated all my efforts on showing them how talented I was so that they would always take me seriously from the get-go. If I could prove my abilities they would be less apt to look at me as a sexual object because career was just as important as sex for most of them.

Unfortunately, talent can also be an aphrodisiac at times. At least it was for this particular artist. I was introduced to him by Tommy Mottola (another early believer in me who helped me tremendously in establishing myself as a go-to songwriter). Tommy had told him about my songwriting chops. This artist was currently starting a new album and Tommy thought that a writing trip including me, the artist, and his longtime producer/writer would help yield the perfect mix of songs. I was sent off that morning with marching orders to "write some fucking hits." And I was ready and happy to comply. This was a huge deal and I knew it. This artist was at the height of his career and I wanted to climb to great heights, too.

Of course, guys this famous never traveled without bodyguards (although body guards are often nothing more than buffed-up family members). So it's the three of us creatives and a couple of big burly guys all headed to a remote ski lodge in upstate New York. I assumed that when we got there, we'd be joined by a cook, a maid, the star's wife, his mother, ANYONE. I was wrong. Not only was I the only woman in this cabin located in the woods, but there was just one private bedroom and five or so cots set up in a common room on the lower level. To make matters worse, the guys played a joke on me, telling me that using cell phones was strictly prohibited because it interfered with the creative process. I had to turn mine off so there were no incoming or outgoing calls. Wow. How was I going to make it through three days like this? I wasn't scared until it was time for bed on the first night and this totally doted-upon star kept hovering in the one bedroom he had previously offered to me. Of course, he was hoping for some extracurricular activity since we'd been cooped up all day writing. But I wasn't going to be his thirty minutes or so of cardio exercise. I kept telling him that I had a boyfriend until he got so tired of hearing it that he retreated.

The next few days were incredibly uncomfortable. He had some nerve taking a woman up there with so many other men under those conditions. All I wanted to do was write songs. Instead, the trip's activities consisted of watching Russian porn, scavenging around the kitchen for food, leering at two strippers (who had braved a blizzard to get there from New York City) as they performed sex acts in the living room, and, oh yeah, writing music. I could have sued Sony for millions of dollars over the sexist shit I endured on that trip, but my career was on an upswing and I wanted to see how far I could take it. I was concerned that if I reported any of this it would affect my new relationship with the record company and the promise of working with true professionals like Céline Dion.

While this star never touched me up to this point, he created a hellish environment for me to work in during the weeks that followed. Because our next writing trip took place on a tropical island, my boyfriend came along as protection. Needless to say, the egomaniac I was writing for wasn't happy to see him. He interpreted my actions as some sort of sick challenge. He was used to having any model he wanted, so who was this civilian chick, this writer who wouldn't mess with him? As bad as his harassment got, I had decided that I wasn't gonna let this bastard deter me from doing the job that Tommy had entrusted to me. Fuck him, I was gonna protect myself with every resource available to me, even if that meant taking my boyfriend with me on every subsequent trip.

While we were traveling, this nightmare of a star was treated like a god. Everywhere we went, beautiful women threw themselves at him. He would be speaking to one of them, and the next thing you knew, they would be in the bathroom fooling around while two of his BGs guarded the door. It was sickening, especially because I knew he had a wife and child. His wife was so sweet. I once told her that I loved a pair of pants she had on (they were really unique—they were black with strings around the knees and they flared out at the bottom). The next time I saw her she gave me the exact same pair of pants as a gift. When she handed them to me, I wanted to cry and tell her what an animal she was married to. But I think she knows this by now, as they have long since divorced.

The situation really got out of control, though, on the last night of our writing for the record. The producer and I took a car service from the city to this star's house in the suburbs. This producer suffered from narcolepsy, which meant that he could fall asleep anytime, anywhere, so I shouldn't have been surprised when he was out like a light within the first few hours of the session. This was lecher boy's opportunity. He shamelessly chased me around his basement with his wife and child upstairs sleeping. At one point, he grabbed my hand and put it on his penis, and that's when I had enough. I was in tears when I woke up Sleeping Beauty, the producer, and told him to call the car. I had to leave. I was really shaken up and had had it.

The next day I went into Tommy's office to discuss the matter, but by then he had already heard about it. He said, "I'm sorry about what happened. The guy's got a real problem."

I explained how he'd terrorized me and told him exactly what had happened.

"What did you do?" he asked.

"I looked him straight in the eye and said, 'Are you done now? Can we finish the song?'"

And Tommy and I never spoke of it again.

By the way, karma is a bitch. The man's record did not live up to its grand expectations, probably because he recorded most of the material in one night after drinking several six-packs of beer and smoking back-to-back cigarettes, which is hell on anybody's voice. Even though I was partially responsible for his album, I must admit our songs were not great. I always like to do my best work on every project I'm assigned, but there simply was no way to write great music under those conditions. I vowed never to work like that again, and thankfully I've never encountered a hellish work environment like that since.

Now, I want to be absolutely certain that no one walks away after reading this chapter thinking that I, for one second, condone sexual harassment or date rape, or that I think you should just suck it up and move on if God forbid it happens to you. ABSOLUTELY NOT. The choice as to how to deal with such events is a deeply personal matter, but for me, back then, music was my lifeline. The thought of not being able to continue on my musical journey was more devastating to me than what had transpired between me and any of these men. My fear of being thrown out of the industry or of being treated like a leper, which is a consequence that happens all too often to women who do blow the whistle, scared the hell out of me. These events affected me greatly. It was difficult for me to relay them here and to be specific about details that I've long since buried somewhere deep inside where they can't get to me as much anymore. But the anguish always resurfaces. Thankfully, I now have the strength to let the truth out no matter what the consequences may be.

Fortunately, most of the men I worked with have valued my talent so they concentrated on how I could better the music and their career. In fact, they were more apt to act like mama bears with their baby cub, protecting me against the wild frontier that the music business tends to so often be. In some cases, it may have taken a minute for the male artist to realize that I was good at my job. Since working with a woman in this field was so rare, they had to see for themselves that I took business as seriously as they did. I think men's fascination with my ballsy, no-fear exterior may have hooked them, but the smart ones were ultimately interested in what I could do creatively. The lesson in all of this: always lead with your talent and eventually people will see that they can gain infinitely more from that than whatever else they may have had in mind.

Reflections on Writing "I Do Not Hook Up" with Katy Perry

Working with Katy Perry is like trying to capture and contain raw creative energy in a bottle. She is electric, feisty, and ultratalented. I respect her mostly for her drive and her resolve to never let rejection keep her down. Early in her career Katy was dropped from labels and probably wrote hundreds of songs for albums that were never released, but she didn't give up. I'd like to believe that when you have that sort of talent and work ethic, you ultimately win, and she did.

"I Do Not Hook Up" was a song she had cowritten with Greg Wells. For whatever reason, she didn't like the original chorus. She came over to my house so we could both take a stab at it. It all just kind of came together. The song is about casual sex, and Katy and I ended up finishing it on the kitchen floor, which, when you think about it, seems amusing. I fell in love with the verses. Katy has this way of speaking that is so unique to her and utterly colloquial. She is blessed with a knack for great melodies, too, and the combination is a winning one. She had the title, so all we had to do was create a great melody and think logically about what she was saying. We threw ideas around and came up with: "Oh no, I do not hook up, I go slow, so if you want me, I don't come cheap, keep your thing in your pants, your heart on your sleeve." "Oh no, I do not hook up, I go slow, so the more that you try, the harder I'll fight to say good night."

Man I'd been saying that to men my whole life. It felt good to finally put it to music. It was empowering.

And then we worked on a bridge. I still have the original demo with Katy singing it. For some reason she did not use it on her album and when I saw her the day she judged on *Idol* Season 9 in California, she told me she was glad she didn't put it on her record since "it wasn't a hit." It actually was a hit as it went top ten on the charts but I guess when you have a string of number ones that kind of placement pales in comparison. I had never known Katy to have so much bite and moxie as she did during the filming of the show that day, but I thought she was fun and entertaining. I'm a fan. Whenever I walk by a newsstand and see her on the cover of a magazine, I always smile. I know what she went through to get to where she is, and when she finally got her break, she was prepared.

The song was recorded by Kelly Clarkson, who did a great job with it on her fourth studio album. She didn't want to sing the line "keep your thing in your pants, your heart on your sleeve," so she changed it to "keep your head in my hands, your heart on your sleeve." She cleaned it up for the world. Maybe she was onto something.

Eight

WALK AWAY

"You need to know this situation's getting old
and now the more you talk
the less I can take . . ."

**eople say** you either fall for some-
one like your father or someone who
is the complete opposite of him. You
become accustomed to the behavior of
your parents and the way they negoti-
ate their relationship. You seek out what's familiar.
In my case, I dated a lot men who were workaholics
and driven like my dad and they triggered in me
those same old feelings of needing to prove that I
was deserving of love. I desperately wanted these
men's attention and adoration, but after a while I got
sick of spending all my energy on what I now know
to be a futile task. When a person can't love you the
way you need and deserve to be loved (not neces-

sarily "want to be loved" because sometimes we want what isn't at all what we need or deserve), MOVE ON—or, rather, walk the hell away. There IS someone out there who can and will love you the way you were intended to be loved. The question is, are you ready for them? Have you done the necessary work on yourself to prepare for them? And, just as important, can you handle their admiration, which, when you're not used to it, can feel really strange? If you can, then don't expect them to be what you imagined when they do finally come along. Trust me, they may not be.

My father suffers from OWD (meaning Overachieving Workaholics Disease—a term I came up with to describe the condition he and all other Type As have), which is great for accomplishing things but can interfere with the time commitment needed for being a great parent. I suffer from it as well, but strive for balance and understand the costs of allowing my drive to dominate my personal life. My father was the product of immigrant parents and the American Dream. His reality and mine were polar opposites. His father came from Italy with nothing and barely spoke English. My grandmother, although born here, was also poor, as her mother left her wealthy family in Italy to marry a peasant. My dad had the pressure of being the first-born son, which in Italian families, like many others, means you better do something big with your life. I was the first born, too, and despite very obviously being a girl, he made do, treating me like I had a Y chromosome, too! He was expected to excel as a kid and so was I. How he felt about the pressure put upon him and whether he wanted to be the golden child or not didn't matter. He didn't have a choice. His parents were in survival mode, making sure that there was enough food on the table. They sacrificed what little they had so my dad and their other children could have more in life and achieve what they couldn't. My dad's feelings seemed unimportant next to their desire to make sure their children made a mark in the world.

As a result, my father has never been an emotional kind of guy. I only saw him cry once in my life and that was when his mother died. Naturally, he never legitimized my feelings and up until recently never said he was sorry as I am not sure he's comfortable with his own emotions. He buried himself in work, and at times it was so bad that I had to schedule appointments to see him. So I never really got the warm, cozy feelings I wanted from him.

Now, I don't want anyone to think that I don't respect and love my father. I do, but our relationship has never been easy. We have many common traits, which is probably why we butt heads so often. He helped me to become the headstrong, ballsy, no-nonsense, work-your-ass-off-and-never-say-you-can't-do-it person I am today. And for that, I owe him a lot. Without his example I would not have been able to achieve my dreams. In my business, hard work and being able to handle rejection are key factors in succeeding. My dad showed me through his example how to work through challenges and to always hold my head up high, which really helped me through difficult times. I may have worried that he didn't think the things I did were ever good enough, but deep down I know he believed I was capable of greatness, so I believed it, too. And believing you are capable of something is half the battle.

I have a favorite and vivid memory of dancing with my dad in our living room when I was young (I teared up just now thinking about it). He was carrying me and singing a Frank Sinatra song in my ear. I was so happy. He was my hero. He was powerful and strong, a deep contrast to my mother, who at the time I felt was negative and weak. Every night at ten or so, I would wait at the top of the stairs for him to come home from New York City. I had missed him and his positive energy. In those early days he made me feel like I could do anything, and more important, he'd promised to bring me a Chunky candy bar, which was one of my first sweet addictions.

As a kid, you know when something is wrong in your family even if you don't know exactly what it is. And in those moments, you don't necessarily understand that a marriage is a complex relationship. While I wasn't able to understand why my parents were unhappy, I could sense it.

I didn't comprehend then that my father's nonstop working and my mother's self-imposed confinement to bed all day were their ways of coping with an unfulfilling marriage. They were a mismatch from the start, and being Catholic screwed them up even more as they should have been able to cut their losses and divorce way before having kids—although I am happy they did not because I love my life and I adore my brother even more and I can't imagine being on this earth without him. But Catholics stay together, and so that's what my parents did.

My parents gave us a lot. A great home, great schools, ballet lessons, vacations, and way more material things than most people in the world ever get. In that regard I was lucky and blessed. But I can honestly say I never saw them kiss passionately. I never saw one sneak up behind the other for a hug or whisper something romantic in the other's ear. I wish I could remember myself saying "Ewwwww, that's so gross, stop kissing," which is what my stepdaughter Elora screams when she's around my husband and me.

For that I felt great sadness. Not for me, but for them. How horrible to have been in a marriage where those moments did not exist. Thankfully, my father has found that with my wonderful stepmother, Shirley, who has been a great influence on all our lives.

You would think that adults would recognize the issues in their marriage and work on them. But when their problems are more about the fundamental differences between them, it's almost impossible to fix. My mother was laid-back, and if the house was a mess, or her drawers were in complete chaos, she was fine with it. My father, on the other hand, was a neat freak who insisted on order. They approached situations differently. My father would scream and yell when he was upset. My mother would withdraw and internalize. She found peace in looking at the water—ponds, rivers, lakes, streams, the sea—and enjoying a leisurely phone call with a friend. My father was a doer who always juggled multiple projects at once. Working hard made him feel good about himself (which is something I can relate to). For years, my parents tried to change each other and it never worked because you can't change people. You can only work on yourself.

Naturally, the first relationships I got into were all fraught with great obstacles and mirrored the mismatching of my parents' marriage. Take for example, my first crush, whom I met at day camp when I was twelve. He was Jewish (which poses problems when you are Catholic) and from

New Jersey (which is geographically undesirable when you can't drive). My mother nixed the whole "friendship" when he called and asked if I wanted to go to the movies. Plus, I was definitely a little too young for a full-fledged boyfriend.

Then there was my first love and the guy I lost my virginity to. I was fifteen and he was almost seventeen. We met at the dance bar Tammany Hall on North Avenue in New Rochelle, New York. I still can't figure out how I convinced my parents to let me out that late at night, but I did. I was standing outside the club on the corner (no, I was not hooking) and I saw this ridiculously hot guy. It was a scene out of a movie because it felt as if the waters parted right there in front of me like the Red Sea did for Moses. *It was love at first sight.* Of course it was; he was older, not Catholic, from a divorced family, lived in a different town, and during his teen years was a bit of a "bad boy." I sought out a relationship full of issues and drama from the get-go because it felt very familiar to me.

For whatever reason, he had to leave shortly after our brief encounter and I wasn't sure if I'd ever see him again. On that Monday afternoon I was sitting in the library at the school with one of my closest friends, Liz, telling her all about him and out of nowhere he walks in with two of his buddies. I was mortified because I was wearing the same clothes I wore the night I met him and I wasn't wearing any makeup (that's how we rolled at my all-girls high school; who cared what we looked like). My friend jumped up and hid in the book stacks because according to her she looked like crap, too. His friends were giving him sideways glances as if to say, *This is the girl you had to track down and find? What are you, crazy?* To his credit, he must have still liked me, because he called me that night and the night after.

What drew me to him was his darkness. He was reeling from the breakup of his parents. He wore it like a leather jacket that he never took off. In fact, he actually wore a leather jacket and drove a motorcycle and was exactly the kind of guy my parents wanted me to be with—*not*. Even though my parents were still married, I was feeling a lot of the same emotions he was because of the tension between them. Being around him made me feel edgier and cool, but more important, it got me thinking about my own family situation and my parents' belief system. It seemed hypocritical to be religious and still shun someone because he wasn't of the same faith or because his parents were divorced. Wasn't one of the commandments to love thy neighbor as thyself? If we abided by that rule, there would be no wars. I wanted desperately to rebel, but I was too scared of my father to do anything extreme. I would have been in serious trouble and this fear definitely kept me out of many questionable teenage activities.

When it came to sex, this boyfriend was way more advanced than I was. I was so inexperienced that I thought giving a blow job meant blowing on a penis till it got hard. Imagine trying that out on your first love? I was down there awhile when he asked me what I was doing and proceeded to give me a lesson I'll never forget. He had had lots of sex before meeting me and clearly wanted more. I thought I was going to go to hell if I did it, but he was going to be there, too, so at least it would be worth it. One day after school we went over to his town house (his mother worked, so she usually wasn't home until around six) and we did it on his couch in the basement. I was staring at my watch nervously the whole time because I was keeping my friend Anne waiting outside; she was my ride and I knew she needed to get home to study. It sucked. I did it for him, not for me.

It was the only time we slept together until I was nineteen.

Of course confession followed this whole debauchery and the key to making it through this process was to spread out the sins over many visits. If I told the priest too many sins or a big one like sex before marriage, the number of Our Fathers and Hail Marys in my penance would take so long that my parents would surely know I was up to no good. When I finally told the priest what I had done, he said, "You are now no longer a flower and no man will want you."

Number one, I had never *been* a flower, and number two, I don't know what planet he lived on, but weren't girls who put out the most wanted of all?

That day was the day that in my heart I stopped being Catholic. I've never gotten the whole confess-to-a-priest-to-get-to-God thing anyway. After that experience, I figured I'd just talk to the Big Guy directly, thank you.

The priest wasn't the only person who had known about me losing my virginity. My father had overheard me talking on the phone, and instead of confronting me about the experience, he just assumed I was sexually active with the entire neighborhood. So he hated this boyfriend and any other guy who came within a twenty-mile radius of me. Of course, I wasn't having sex with him. He had moved on to having sex with one of my friends, unbeknownst to me, and when I found out I was devastated. That broke us up but started an on-again, off-again pattern that eventually ended when he converted to Christianity and married. How's that for irony? (We actually reconnected a few months back through Facebook and I am happy to report that we've both gotten our shit together since high school and he's become a great man.)

After him, I rebounded by dating boring/nice men who made me feel dead inside. I never felt THAT connection, that spark, and the crazy, creative side of me became stifled as a result. I should have had the courage to walk away, but I felt safe in those kinds of relationships, and that safety sort of lulled me into complacency. I hurt some of these men deeply and for that I am truly sorry (if any of you are reading this). I only felt alive when I was with someone who made me want to prove my worth, someone I had to change or save in some way, someone who was as fucked up as or more fucked up than me. These were all terrible foundations for a relationship. So there was my pendulum, and it swung like that for years between nice, safe, boring men and insecure, damaged, emotionally unavailable ones.

In most of the tumultuous relationships I've been in, there were always signs that disaster was ahead, but I chose to ignore them because I was more focused on my career. That was always my priority, in the same way that it seemed to often be my father's. To stop and acknowledge the issues would have taken time and it was easier to just pretend the issues didn't exist. I also liked the shield of having a boyfriend. At a certain age, when you are unmarried and not dating anyone, people start to think you must be half off your rocker. I laugh now at how naive I was to think that any of these relationships could have amounted to anything when I was working all the time and fitting in my boyfriends like I did mani/pedis. You have to put into a relationship what you expect to get out of it.

After my mother died, I got into the worst relationship of my life, probably because I was in the worst head space of my life. Of course, it was long distance—and not just a few hours by car. I'm talking bodies of water between us, as in "he lived in another country." I had been traveling back and forth to Sweden, which was a center for pop music at the time. The movement was started by the late, great Dennis Pop, who produced and wrote such songs as "Show Me Love" by Robyn. Before he died, he mentored Max Martin (one of the greatest producer/songwriters alive today). Max started a musical revolution with his team of producer/writers and went on to pen mega hits such as Britney's "Hit Me Baby One More Time," the Backstreet Boys' "I Want It That Way," and 'N Sync's "Tearing Up My Heart." For a young songwriter with an extreme fear of flying due to having endured a few emergency landings (I used to make my brother go with me on my first flights to Sweden), international travel on a regular basis was not ideal. But I knew that I had to be around these writers to soak up their genius. I've often thought that Swedes are such good writers because they speak in melody.

During one of my trips, I met an executive in the Swedish music market. Note: There was no overlap there because I wasn't trying to get my records on Swedish radio. I was simply trying to learn more from their process so I could go back and conquer the States with my newfound knowledge. I was immediately attracted to the bad boy in this man. He was bald, tattooed, and so not right for me. True to my modus operandi, I thought I could save him. Meanwhile I was the one who needed saving. The fact that we lived in two different countries was appealing. It enabled us to work very long hours and then take minivacations together. But you never truly get the full sense of someone this way. It's too much like a perpetual honeymoon. As soon as something goes wrong, you're leaving in a few days anyway.

When he started to experience a downswing in his career in Sweden, he decided to move into the U.S. market. I introduced him to Tommy Mottola, who gave him a consultancy job at Sony. The next time I was in Sweden, however, I noticed a newspaper on his kitchen counter with his and Tommy Mottola's names in the headline. Of course I couldn't read the article since it was written in Swedish, but it seemed like he had told everyone that Tommy Mottola had sought him out and hired him, which made him look like a superstar. He was playing me, but I refused to acknowledge the warning signs.

Soon after, we got engaged. He gave me diamond earrings as a gift. I no longer have the diamonds, but I still have the three-times-the-normal-size hole in my left earlobe that resulted when an allergy to the posts caused the piercing to stretch. My husband begs me to get it fixed, but I refuse because I never want to forget what it was like to be with the wrong person.

Before I knew enough to part ways with my Swedish beau, I tried to help him resolve some financial troubles he was having. We were, after all, going to be married, so lending him $100K seemed like the right thing to do. At the extreme urging of my extraordinary lawyer, Jaimie Roberts, who has always protected me and has been with me throughout my career, I took his jewelry as collateral. (I didn't want to do that, but I had never seen Jaimie so adamant about anything.) What the hell was I doing with a guy who wore diamond jewelry anyway?! A few months later one of my best friends, Michelle, was in Sweden when a very young woman tapped her on the shoulder and introduced herself as my fiancé's girlfriend. As soon as my friend gave me the 411, I called my lawyer and had him send a letter of direction garnishing the bastard's wages at Sony until he paid me back every cent of my $100K plus interest, which he did. Breaking my heart was one thing, but there was no way he was going to walk away with my hard-earned money. While I had been taken, it was my own fault, too. I should have listened to him when he said he would never be happy with someone more successful than himself. I am sure there are many people reading this book who have faced challenges in their relationships because they are in a better professional position than their partners. It's an unfair insecurity that can ruin a relationship. In this case, I'm glad it did.

Now, I do believe that God breaks it all down for you until you finally understand your own behavior, at which time you can decide either to fix it or to let it destroy you. Luckily my profession was a great tool in my recovery from these relationships. Writing songs had always been an outlet for my pain, disappointment, and fear of being alone, and this was especially true at this time. Writing forced me to look at what I was doing to myself and see how destructive my choices had become. I didn't even know how angry I was until I started writing songs like Kelly Clarkson's "I Hate Myself for Losing You" and "Walk Away," and Theory of a Deadman's "Not Meant to Be." In fact, I didn't even know how bad it was until I reread the lyrics. Living in my feelings was key to my recovery and my later avoidance of these types of relationships. True, I had come back from an eating disorder, but I still had issues with destructive behavior, and these relationships were proof of it.

I also think I stayed in these relationships because they gave me something to write about. They fueled my creativity. How many times do you love an artist's early music only to be disappointed by it when they become happy, fall in love, and get rich? I subconsciously thought that my music might suffer in the same way if I was happy. While I love Pablo Picasso's words "All creation comes from devastation," I would learn that you don't need to stay in the chaos to create art . . . all you need is your memory.

Here I am as a child with my mom, dad, and brother, John . . .

with my mom on my birthday (I couldn't wait to get my hands in that cake) . . .

with my paternal grandparents and John at our summer home . . .

and all of us with my mom's parents, Nanny Mary and Papa John. I miss them every day.

This is me singing for guests at Christmastime . . .

with Johnny and our overfed cats who were almost as big as us . . .

trying to avoid the camera during my bingeing days . . .

all grown up with John . . .

and with my dad and former New Jersey governor Thomas Kean at a political function. I think I sang at that event, too.

This is me with my bandmates from
Gramma Trips . . .

with Jon Wolfson when we were the duo
known as Mad Doll . . .

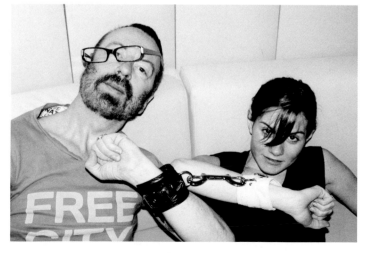

and with Dave
Stewart in our
Platinum Weird days.
He and I had an
instant connection.
Can you tell?

This is me with Larry Flick, former dance editor at *Billboard,* a dear friend and my first big champion . . .

with former Warner Bros. chairman and CEO Tom Whalley and the legendary David Foster . . .

with Gabe Saporta of Cobra Starship . . .

with Christina Aguilera and my business partner Stephen Finfer. . .

with Gary LeVox and Jay DeMarcus of the Rascal Flatts . . .

and with Colbie Caillat at the beach house in Hawaii where we wrote "I Never Told You" and other songs. It was like being at camp but better.

Here I am with the Bee Gees and Sean Garrett the night we won Songwriter of the Year at the BMI Awards . . .

with Katy Perry after her *Idol* appearance . . .

and with Pink and two-time Grammy-nominated producer and songwriter Gregg Wells after a writing session.

This photo was taken after my acting debut with Hannah Montana . . .

with one of my favorite *Idol* contestants, Kelly Clarkson . . .

with Randy Jackson and Jaime Roberts (because every girl needs a dawg and a lawyer),

with Simon Cowell, who always made weird faces at me . . .

with Kris Allen and Adam Lambert, who thankfully forgave me for "No Boundaries" . . .

and with Ryan and Katrina (aka Bikini Girl). *What am I, insane?!*

Yes, this is me sobbing after the Season 8 finale (I had been holding back tears from the very first show!) . . .

hugging one of my favorite people, Vera Wang, whom I met during *Idol* . . .

and in the photo I will never live down—our first group picture and the last time I will ever wear leopard print.

had fun hanging in my dressing room with Neil Patrick Harris, who created and wore this T-shirt to the show . . .

and was thrilled to meet The Fonz, Henry Winkler, by chance at the airport. It was great to discover that he liked me on *Idol*!

This is me and Katherine McPhee dueting at a Phoenix House event . . .

with four promising award winners at the Phoenix House recording studios Arthouse built . . .

and with real-life saint Sister Domingues, who runs the orphanage I visited in Africa as part of Idol Gives Back.

This is me singing "Ain't No Other Man" to my husband at our wedding . . .

and us on the beach that day. I'm wearing my mother's wedding dress.

love this photo of me, Mike, and my dog Tikki . . .

this cozy one with my stepdaughter, Elora, and godson, Michael . . .

and this one with my goddaughter, Cami.

It was hilarious when Elora dressed
Mike up for Halloween. Clearly, I dig
rocker boys.

This is my amazing second mom,
Marianne Dowling . . .

my dad, me, and
lovely stepmom
Shirley.

These are some of my bffs—Suzie
and Liz . . .

and more of them lounging around
watching *Law and Order* with me
on my thirty-seventh birthday.
Pictured from left to right: Suzie,
Becky, me, and Angie.

Finally, this is me with Mitch Allan at one of my live concerts, where the idea for this book
was born . . .

with Jason Derulo and Ryan Seacrest after guesting on Ryan's radio show . . .

and chilling at a sound
check. . . . See you at one
of my performances!

Reflections on Writing "Walk Away" with Kelly Clarkson

Writing "Walk Away" was like pulling teeth. Hit songs usually come fast for me. When inspiration enters the room, it's usually a thirty-minute window in which the majority of the song is created. Not on this day. I was working with a husband-and-wife team, which can sometimes be challenging. My creative connection with the husband was stronger than with his wife despite the fact that she is very talented. He and I had a similar sensibility and in our sessions it seemed as if he liked my ideas more, which made it awkward for me. We must have been at it for an hour, and nada. At one point she took a break and bingo, that's when the first hints of the song started coming to us. When she returned we all finished it together except for the bridge. My lyrical contribution to the song had a lot to do with the last relationship I was in before I met my husband. I'm not even gonna go there about this relationship because it was the moral low point of my life, and to this day, I beat myself up for it. The guy was married, though thankfully no one (but the two of us) got hurt. Let's keep it that way by not getting into any details except to say that I walked away.

One of the greatest things about this song was having Kelly Clarkson record it. Having her sing anything of yours is like bringing an old piece of furniture to the refinisher. When you get it back it's been brought to life. She's one of my favorite artists and people. The moment I met her, I fell in love. She was feisty, honest, real, and generous. She has this gift of putting her soul into her voice, and she gave women the best piece of advice when she wrote the bridge of the song:

I want a love, I want a fire to feel the burn of my desire
I want a man by my side, not a boy who runs and hides
Are you gonna fight for me, die for me, live and breathe for me
Do you care for me, 'cause if you don't then just leave.

I've always had one regret about this song. As writers, we are always under the gun to finish things quickly, sometimes so quickly that we miss noticing something until it's too late . . . like when the song is on the radio. I would have rewritten the first line to be "I'm looking for intention, not another question" as opposed to "I'm looking for attention, not another question." As women, we need more than just attention; we need to know that someone is committed to us when we're at our most awesome and when we're really being a bitch. Now, if only I had known all that before I went on my first date.

Nine

RICH GIRL

"If I were a rich girl . . ."

have always had an affinity for money and many times it's been the deciding factor when making choices in my career. When I was younger, currency came in the form of Halloween candy. Tootsie Rolls and Crunch bars could be used as payment for the neighborhood kids to take part in a play I had written or as incentive for my brother to get me something from my room and bring it to me. I would keep my Halloween candy for months and ration it out as I saw fit. The key was to always have a reserve of the hard candy that wouldn't go stale. Six months after trick-or-treating, my Halloween "money" was still good.

At a certain age you realize that in order to have

some freedom from your parents, you've got to have your own cash. At ten years old, I would spend hours after school selling Christmas stamps or shoveling snow. I loved the feeling of money in my hands. It enabled me to make choices, and choices back then were few and far between. You ate what your parents cooked for you, you wore what they bought you, and you went where they told you to go. I was sick of waiting around for Christmas to see which great-aunt would give me a ten-dollar bill, although I did appreciate their generosity. It's just that I wanted to make my own money . . . and fast.

As I mentioned earlier, my first job was at a chocolate-and-gelato shop in Scarsdale, New York, called Enjou. I had convinced my parents that working there would be a good experience for me. My father liked the idea, since he had stacked cans on the shelves of his parents' grocery store before and after school while he was growing up. But my mother worried that the job would interfere with my schoolwork. Also, nobody else's kids were working, nor did we have to. But I didn't care about the impression it may have left. I was too concerned with attaining financial freedom. That's all that really mattered.

We lived in a beautiful house, took vacations, drove nice cars. But for some reason, my mother never had any money. My dad had underestimated how far you could go on two hundred dollars a week. It was frustrating for me to watch my mother have to explain where all the money had gone and ask for more. It shifted the power in the relationship to my father. Although my father had a reason to keep his eye on her spending since my mother had maxed out all their credit cards early in their marriage, it was still disheartening to see my mother beholden to my father for money. My dad was the bank, my mother was the loanee, and when you borrow money from the bank, there's always some form of payback (like a kiss or having to act a certain way). I swore to myself at a young age that I would always have my own savings. I would marry whomever I *wanted* to marry, not just someone I *needed* to marry because I was dependent on him.

But my parents weren't the only ones who taught me about money management. I learned a painful lesson when it came time to buy my first car. My maternal grandparents, having been children of the Depression era, were very financially conservative. From the time I was little, I had heard stories about the Great Depression and the stock-market crash. Both my nanny Mary and grandpa John came from wealthy parents whose financial situation was seriously affected by the crash. To this day, I am wary of the financial markets and put most of my money in real estate—I like that I can touch it.

Each year for Christmas my grandparents gave my brother and me Disney bonds to ensure that we would have enough money set aside for our college educations. But all I cared about was turning eighteen and accessing the account to buy a car (which was never what the money was intended for). When I told my father that I wanted to sell the bonds to buy a used Saab, he was totally opposed to it, but had to acquiesce since the money was now in my control. It would take a few days to settle the transaction so to avoid losing the car to another buyer while the funds freed up, I asked my grandmother to advance me the money. She gave me her checkbook and I wrote the man who was selling the car a check from it. When, a short time later, he told me that the check had not cleared, I wrote another. (He must have noticed how happy I was to write checks from a checkbook that wasn't mine.)

Well, it turned out that the guy was a grifter. He had sold my car to ten other people and cashed both of my grandmother's checks and was well on his way to Florida before any of us knew. I was lucky to be the one who got the car in the end, probably because I was the only one who paid double for it. Lesson Number One: No matter how honest someone seems (and this guy seemed totally honest to me, with a family and house in ritzy Bedford Hills, New York), they can potentially screw you. I later found out that not only was the house rented, but the kids were, too. To this day, no one but me writes or signs my checks, and if anyone is handling my investments, they better make sure to run everything by me before making a move. Not a month goes by that some credit-card company doesn't try to charge me for some program I supposedly enrolled in and am not.

As children, we are not raised to think about when we will have money of our own. This is especially true of women. I remember my first house closing. I almost had a heart attack when I saw the documents. There was no way I could sign the paperwork without reading it, but reading it left me in a state of real confusion and anxiety. I didn't understand any of it and asked a million questions until I could see the lender praying the deal would fall through. NO one ever taught me about mortgages, stocks, bonds, or money markets. And as we all found out during the housing crisis of the past few years, it's often a big set up that leaves you over leveraged and out of control of what you thought were your assets. Half the time you don't even understand the lingo that they're throwing around. My advice is to know exactly where your money is going to and use your common sense. If someone tells you that you will make a crazy return on your investment or that you can take large sums of money out against your property, chances are there is a high risk or interest rate involved.

I also subscribe to the motto "don't buy it if you can't pay for it outright." Live beneath your means. We are all spending money we don't have, including the government. (My dad runs an informative not-for-profit foundation called Truth in Government. You should check it out.) Financial stress is a disease. It seeps into all areas of your life and wreaks havoc—on your relationships, your soul, your creativity and productivity. Now, I am not saying you should pay for your house in cash. All I am saying is that knowing you could do so or that you have a large enough amount of money in reserve as padding keeps you financially sound, which will allow you to sleep well at night and concentrate your efforts on being the best you can be.

Because I like being in control of my assets, I always knew I would own a business. K'Stuff, my original catalog of songs, was, for all intents and purposes, my first business. I didn't come up with the name. Brian Brinkerhoff, a music executive who was funding my first independent CD, wrote the name on a cassette box and it stuck. In some ways this catalog was like a stock portfolio. There were some songs that spiked the value of the business as they catapulted up the charts, like Hilary Duff's "Come Clean" and others that, so to speak, didn't deliver the expected dividends such as "With

Love." Because I had saved up enough money to live on during the years I worked at *Billboard*, I never had to sell the rights to my catalog, which would have been like needing a partner to fund your business because you couldn't do it on your own. I only gave others the right to collect on it for a period of time. I could do this because I was never in a fiscally unstable position. I had an education and money in the bank that I had earned to fall back on. I have learned that you never want to make decisions in your life when you are in a weakened financial position or you are tired. (I have found that people can be very emotional when they don't have sleep.) I have also learned that if you are a hard worker you will always want to bet on yourself. It's the people who stay in the game and work intensely who win in the long run.

I can honestly say I am one of the hardest working people in my industry and that above everything else, this has been the key to my success. In the beginning my friends used to joke that I was the hardest-working girl NOT in show business. As I said before, I got my work ethic from my father. I never saw the man take a day off in his life. He gave 100 percent every-day and never made excuses for why he couldn't achieve something. In his mind, anything was possible as long as you worked hard enough, even being elected to Congress. He left his esteemed position as a partner at Arthur Andersen to pursue a career in politics. Everyone thought he was nuts and that he wouldn't win the election. The man got up at four o'clock every morning for months to go to train stations and worked until twelve at night. His battery never ran out. He won the election and served in Congress for four years. In this last New York senatorial election, the party bosses did not back him at the convention level, but he knew the public would. He secured fifty thousand signatures from voters so he could run in a primary, and he won. I got my "If you tell me I can't do it, just watch me" attitude from him. He lost the election, but considering his opponent outspent him ten to one, he made a great showing. (P.S. I'm a registered Independent.)

Most of my songs that appear on albums are placements I secured. For years, I never had a manager or agent and while people introduced me to some of my most lucrative writing partners, I knew how to sell my songs both through my voice and at times with my very aggressive nature. I never let an opportunity pass me by.

I remember my first meeting with Tommy Mottola at the height of his Sony success. He had gotten a copy of Enrique Iglesias's unmastered *Escape* album from someone (I'd rather not say who) and wanted to meet the team behind it. Of course, giving Tommy an unreleased record from a competitive label was like selling U.S. intelligence to Russia. Realizing the seriousness of his actions after the fact, that idiot who gave it to him was running around Tommy's house trying to find the CD. I thought we were all gonna get thrown out or worse. During the meeting, Tommy zeroed in on me as I was the most normal of the bunch and he was impressed that I had graduated from Duke. A few weeks later I was summoned to his office in the Sony building on 550 Madison Avenue. Back then, this was as big as getting a call to be on *American Idol*. He was a definitive gatekeeper and launched the careers of some of the biggest names in music. I felt an immediate connection with him, maybe because he was Italian like me and I could imagine him at Christmas making a sauce (or rather tasting the sauce his mama had made for him). The meeting lasted only five minutes. Tommy was smart; he knew that taking a meeting with a songwriter (even for thirty seconds) would get that songwriter to work for him for free. For a tunesmith, it was like spending time with the president. His most immediate need was a song for Jessica Simpson. He asked me to keep in touch and to send him anything I might have for her.

I went back to my apartment that night and stayed up until I had written a song (melody and lyrics) called "A Little Bit." The problem was that I was in New York and didn't know any producers who could come up with the chords and put together the right production of the song so I could play it properly for Tommy. At the time I was mostly working with Steve Morales, who was based out of Miami. But I had to show Tommy what I was capable of and how serious I was about creating songs for his artists. There was no way I was going to miss the opportunity to take advantage of this lucky break. So I called his office.

"Hi, this is Kara, the songwriter from yesterday. Tommy—I mean

Mr. Mottola told me he needed a song for Jessica Simpson and well . . . I wrote one."

"Great, please send it to us," his assistant said curtly.

"Yeah, the thing is, I can't send it . . . 'cause it's in my head," I replied.

There was a long pause. Tommy's assistants were used to fielding calls all day long from weirdos trying to get Tommy to listen to their music or come to a show. I knew this because I had dealt with one of Tommy's three assistants when I was at *Billboard* and had to make lunch appointments with Tommy for my old boss. These girls were like pit bulls protecting their master.

"All right, so how is he supposed to hear it, Kara?" The woman was getting impatient as other lines were ringing.

"I need to come sing it for him," I told her. She sighed and put me on hold for what seemed like ten minutes.

"Come right now," she said firmly when she got back on.

Within twenty minutes I was facing Tommy and waiting for my computer to boot up (which felt like it took an eternity) so I could read the lyrics and sing the song. I was so nervous, but knew that if he saw so much as an inkling of fear I was dead. I had made this man stop everything he was doing to listen to my song. If he didn't like it that would be it.

I stood up and began hitting my hip to show him how the beat went and then I sang the entire song. At the end I looked up, and he was almost in a state of shock.

"You wanna be a singer?" he said. "You can really sing."

"No," I replied. "I'm quite happy as a songwriter."

"You're a smart girl. All the money's in the publishing. I LOVE THAT SONG."

"Get me Donnie Ienner!" he screamed to his assistant. Within moments Donnie, the president of Columbia Records at the time, was in the office and they were giving each other a kiss on both cheeks the way Italians do. I resang the whole song for Donnie. He loved it and they put it on hold for Jessica to cut immediately. It went on to be her next single.

I was the best salesperson for my own songs because they came from my heart. When I thought I had one that was perfect for an artist, nothing could stop me from jumping on an executive's desk and singing it the way I did one time to poor L.A. Reid, the president of Island Records. His desk was full of lit candles that began to fall all over the place as I tried to convince him that a song I'd written called "Screwed" would be a hit for Pink. An executive at the meeting finally said, "Umm can you get off the desk before the building burns down."

I have done some crazy things. When I got myself in front of the powers that be, I went for it. I wasn't worried about what they thought by the time I was right in front of them because I had nothing to lose. I wish I could have showed more of this side of me on *Idol*, but somehow this part of my personality didn't fit within the construct of the panel. Instead I pulled more from my mother's debutante ways than my father's street tactics. And I think America would have gotten a kick out of the Joe in me.

My I'm-gonna-make-you-love-my-songs attitude was a far cry from my somberness back in the days when no one recognized my talent and I couldn't get arrested if I tried to. Which brings me to the subject of resiliency, and how important a role it plays in attaining your dreams. I learned one of the greatest lessons on the subject from my father when he lost his second U.S. congressional race in 1988. At six in the morning after the election, I heard all this noise coming from downstairs. It was my father working the phones, telling his supporters that he was doing fine and that he was still committed to making the world a better place. He refused to let failure stop him. He refused to be depressed. I adopted that attitude in my own career because the truth is, your ability to shake off failure is key to your success. That's not to say that you don't stop and reflect on what you could have done better or how you could have changed the outcome or that you don't even shed a few tears in the moment. But after you do all those things, you keep going. I promise, you will always learn more from your failures than from your successes. Those are the lessons that serve you best in the long run.

In the beginning, I think I stayed in music when all the signs were saying not to because the rejection fueled me. After I was done being sad for a moment, I'd get pissed and take the brush-off as a challenge to show everyone that I *could* attain my dream even if they didn't think so. My grandmother also gave me a great piece of advice: "If you want it, take it." I love that saying because it's proactive and it gives *you* the power—no one else.

Anyway, I was so good at getting my songs cut that even when my cowriters on songs had publishers who were supposed to be shopping them, I was the one who inevitably found a home for them. I decided to start my own publishing company, Arthouse Entertainment, in 2004 with Stephen Finfer so I could administer my copyrights and help other creative people build their catalogs.

I met Stephen through Brooke Morrow. Brooke was one of the best publishers I have ever known. She has golden ears and has signed many of today's biggest stars to publishing deals, including Kelly Clarkson and Nelly Furtado. She was the first person to throw down a serious amount of money to administer (not own) my catalog through EMI. She knew Stephen from law school and thought we should meet since Stephen had signed Scott Storch, a hugely successful producer/writer (Gwen Stefani's "Blow Your Mind," Justin Timberlake's "Cry Me a River," and Pink's "Family Portrait"). She not only thought I should write with Scott, she was also playing matchmaker since she thought Stephen and I might like each other.

When we met, Stephen thought I was gay and I thought he was obnoxious. Of course, we ended up dating, but soon realized that we would be better business partners than anything else. One good thing about starting a business with someone you have lived with is that you have a pretty good sense of their business ethics. Stephen and I both wanted to be successful, but not at the cost of others. We built Arthouse on the strict moral principle of helping our writers and artists be the best they could be. We have a genuine desire as publishers to help build creative partnerships for our songwriters with other writers and music executives.

Stephen is to me what René Angélil is to Céline Dion, my biggest believer, supporter, and reality checker. He's a visionary who tells me I am capable of things years before I actually do them. He always told me I would be a household name and I laughed at him. He also points out when I need to step up my game, as he did during *Idol* Season 8. He'll give me the hard truth and isn't scared that I may throw something at him. When I am having a bad day he reminds me of how far I've come and how lucky I am. He also told me to wear a dark bathing suit for the Bikini Girl showdown in case I wet myself onstage. C'mon, where you gonna find a guy with all those skills? (P.S. I did wet myself that night.) I love Stephen like a brother, and he and I are also a great business team. He is the yin to my yang and we complement each other. We have different skill sets, and when you merge them together, it's a perfect combination. In business you always want to find a partner who complements you, and does what you can't do well. Without him, I wouldn't be where I am today.

We started Arthouse in New York City in 2004 and then later moved it into the basement of my house in California in 2005. With one desk for Stephen in an empty room, we began building our roster. The game plan was to leverage my success. If you wanted to work with me, you had to work with me and one of my writers. The artist would invariably fall in love with that writer and a new relationship was formed. I was the broker for talent, and nothing could have made me happier than to see these on-the-rise musicians flourish.

Within three years we were number seven on the top-ten publishers' list, competing against major companies such as EMI and Sony, who had millions of dollars. And we did it all from one room in my house. The upstairs of my home quickly became a hotel, with many of my writers frequently crashing there. We were a family, and families take care of each other. We've grown a lot since then. At one point in 2010 we copublished ten percent of iTunes' top 100 songs with songs written by our writers and performed by artists such as Bruno Mars, Cee Lo Green, B.O.B., Travie McCoy, Flo Rida, and Carrie Underwood, among others. Two of those songs were nominated for Record of the Year and one for Song of the Year at the 2011 Grammys.

In 2007 Tom Whalley (then president of Warner Bros. Records) asked me to join the artists and repertoire team there. The A&R folks, as they are called, are the executives who find artists and sign them to record labels. Tom first saw me in an *Access Hollywood* piece in which the legendary producer David Foster and I were recording Billy Bush. While working with Billy on his vocals, I was adamant that we try a technique I was sure would help. Tom liked that I stood up to David on the segment, and asked me to come in for a meeting. I decided to take the job because it represented an opportunity to gain knowledge in the one area I did not have expertise in yet: how to market and break artists. My attitude is you can always learn no matter how successful you are. I signed Beluga Heights artists Jason Derulo and Iyaz to Warner Bros., as well as Jason Reeves, Susan Justice, Brandy Burnette, and Neon Hitch.

I love being a "rich girl," but it has its downsides, too. Some may refer to me as more of a bitch girl than a rich girl. Unfortunately, being a strong woman who knows what she wants lends itself to being labeled the B word. But in my experience every time someone tells me that some woman is a bitch, it usually means she's just good at her job and is a straight shooter.

One of my favorite examples of this involves Jewel. She and I were once working with a producer/writer who brought in a verse melody and the first few lines of a song. We wrote the song based on his idea. After listening to the demo I recorded while he was lounging at the pool one Saturday afternoon, he decided that he didn't like what we had written and wanted his idea back to use on another artist's upcoming record. In layman's terms, that would be like giving someone a gift and then a week later showing up and saying that you made a mistake and you wanted it returned. It's very unorthodox. To her credit, Jewel didn't fly off the handle like I almost did. Instead, she asked to hear the demo so that she could hopefully hear why the song did not reach its full potential and learn from the experience. As writers, we need the perspective of listening with fresh ears, as there is always something we can take away from a song that can make us better writers. She promised that he could keep his ideas and he, in turn, promised to send her the recording. Unfortunately he did not keep up his end of the deal. Instead, he seemed to be leaving the country without giving her the demo, probably because he feared she would like the song and change her mind. Now, after four days of him not taking her calls, Jewel had had it. On one occasion she could hear him in the background saying, "Tell her I'm not here." She drove over to the studio in the pouring rain to confront the guy. When she rang the doorbell, he left her waiting outside in the rain. What was even more disturbing was that she could be seen on the security camera standing there getting all wet. So she climbed the fence and went around back. By then the producer was hiding in the bathroom while his car had been waiting outside to take him back to London, presumably with the demo in hand. Well, she scoured the place till she found him and then tore him to pieces, using words I don't think she'd like to read in print. She told him it was going to be her mission in life to make sure that the song was released in every country in the world, making it impossible for him to ever reuse his contribution. He, of course, had nothing to say so he offered her an apology in the moment, which couldn't have meant much as he later called her a bitch. No, no, he had it all wrong. Jewel is my hero and this producer, well, calling him an ass doesn't even begin to cover it.

I think the hardest challenge women face is learning how to be tough and fair and still be nurturing and soft. Unfortunately society, especially TV, only allows you to be one of these at a time. I am known to be aggressive in business and even harsh with my critiques as my approach to artist development is tough love. It tends, in my opinion, to make artists even better. But I still have a sensitive side and I still get hurt. It's important that you protect your softness and don't let it harden into walls because a combination of these traits is really the winning formula.

When I was just a struggling songwriter, my life was simple. I had one focus—writing great songs. The uncomplicated nature of my life helped me be creative. As I've gotten more successful, however, that success has pulled me away from that focus. Having money is great. But with money comes considerable responsibility. You have to make sure that you protect your investments. If you buy homes or cars, they need attention. People look at people with money and think they have it better, but that's not necessarily so—it's just a different way to live and one thing it's not is simple. In the end, being financially secure eased my mind, but doing what I love saved my soul. And one thing is for sure: nothing feels better than knowing that everything you have, YOU MADE YOURSELF!

Reflections on Writing "Rich Girl" with Gwen Stefani

I met Gwen Stefani after cowriting "Rich Girl." To this day I think we have spoken a total of fifty words—forty-eight on the phone that day when she told me she liked my ideas and two in the form of a quick hello at Christina Aguilera's baby shower.

I was in a meeting at Jimmy Iovine's when he pulled out the track, which had the chorus already done. It was an old Dr. Dre track. He said he had asked a lot of people to try to come up with a verse melody and a prehook. No one nailed it. So he was asking me what I would do. He played the track and I started singing some melodies and mouthing some lyrics in the prechorus. He asked me to go to the studio and record my ideas, which he would then send to Gwen.

As I mentioned previously, Jimmy had always been supportive of me and was instrumental in introducing me to some of the greatest producers/artists out there today, from Polow da Don to will.i.am, but I never thought Gwen would dig what I had written.

I was driving a few weeks later when the phone rang.

"Please hold for Jimmy Iovine and Gwen Stefani . . ."

I thought, *Yeah, right, is this a joke?* But it was them. Gwen said she liked what I had done and was going to flesh it out more, lyrically.

I'd like to tell you that it was more organic than that, but it wasn't. Sometimes I don't have the privilege of getting to know the artist on a deeper level. But when you're a songwriter for hire, you're happy when the phone rings and the person on the other end tells you you've got a job to do. And while writing some songs doesn't do much for your soul, I'd be lying if I said that getting the check in the end didn't feel really good.

There is no way to end this chapter without speaking about the critical role that friendship plays in ensuring that you are truly a "rich person." The song I wrote with Gwen taps into that sentiment right before the chorus where it speaks about love being of a higher value than money. I need to really emphasize that you can have all the money, cars, houses, shoes, titles, and success in the world, but if there's no one to share it with, you will truly be a poor person. I was fortunate in my life to learn the importance of friends from my mother. I saw how she leaned on them in her day-to-day life and when she faced her death. While I work long hours, I do try to balance them with time for my personal relationships. This has been one of the smarter moves I've made in my life. I have some of the best friends money *can't* buy—Suzie, Liz, Angie, Becky, Michelle, Lisa, Anne, Katherine, Stephen, Larry, Brooke, Marti, Eve, Karen, Mitch, Derek, Clyde, Tara, Bill, Susan, Katy, Nancy, Faye, Michael, Valerie, and Marianne (in no particular order). And of course . . . I feel like a billionaire for having found my husband, Mike . . .

There's an old adage I like: "Show me your friends and I'll tell you who you are." Nothing is truer than this saying. When I'm out with my friends and have had a few too many, I often catch myself staring at them and thinking *Why do you put up with me? You're so awesome; I must be doing something right.* Before there was ever award season swag or finale tickets, they were there championing me, wiping away the tears when my heart was broken, and loving me through it all. Truth is, I could not have made it this far without them. It takes a village to withstand the challenges in this world and they are definitely on the front line of mine.

Ten

AIN'T NO OTHER MAN

"Ain't no other man who can

stand up next to you . . ."

When I arrived in Prospect Harbor, Maine, during the summer of 2007, I was newly single. The name of this town, by the way, is particularly funny considering the outcome of my visit, as you will soon see. I had broken off a painful three-plus-year relationship. It had not been a healthy one, and while I thought this ex was the love of my life and I would die without him, my idea of love was deeply flawed and distorted. I had almost given up on the idea of finding someone to spend the rest of my life with. Being a successful woman posed many problems when dating. In the previous months, I had tried my luck with some Internet dating sites. The men I met were either in awe of my accomplishments (but really wanted someone less type A) or they were trying to get me to listen to their music. Let's just say I didn't meet my Prince Charming on the Internet. The last thing on my mind when I pulled into my house in Maine was romance, and that's usually when it finds you.

I had bought this house four years earlier along with Marianne Dowling, who, as I've already mentioned, was like my second mother when I was growing up. She was in remission from cancer and had always wanted a summer cottage on the coast of Maine. To someone living in Los Angeles, it seemed easier to get to Bora Bora (it actually *is* easier; I went there on my honeymoon) than to the remote coastal town we chose, but I had lost one mother and was in a position to help this one, so I opted to fulfill her dream, no matter how far away the place was. Part of our deal was that she would fix it up and handle its maintenance. But after spending one summer there, she had stopped going. I decided to take a trip to see just what had been done to the place and to decide if it was worth keeping it. I hadn't seen the house since we purchased it.

I pulled up to the nineteenth-century cottage once owned by a sailor captain and was floored when I saw that a brand-new house was being built just fifteen feet away. In a state of shock, I drove down the wrong driveway—not really recalling in my anger which one was mine—and then cut across my new neighbor's lawn. This was my husband Mike's first vision of me. I was too incensed even to realize that he was watching my bizarre behavior. I had gotten out of the car and was engaged in a heated phone conversation with my father about an issue totally unrelated to the house. There was lots of screaming and cursing coming from my end of the phone. Mike later told me that he had heard the two women who owned the house were royal bitches so this behavior only confirmed that for him. But they weren't talking about me. Marianne and her daughter (both lawyers) had contested the property line between our houses in the hope of blocking the new building. (Again, there was that bitch word being used to describe women who were just defending what was theirs.) This was the first I heard of all this. Was I being punished for my good deed?

I stayed away from the new house for the first two days of my visit. I had heard that the builder was the owner, so naturally I assumed that the guy on the roof with the hammer (Mike) was my enemy. I was not ready to face him just yet. I was afraid that I would run my mouth and it would be an irreparably damaging encounter. But during that cooling-off period, I became smitten—not by Mike just yet, but by Maine.

My friends had done an incredible job of renovating the house, turning it into a cozy coastal retreat. Since our backyard abutted the water, it reminded me of the days I had spent watching the ocean with my mother before she died. I felt so close to her there. I could feel her with me.

Maine filled my soul back up with everything it was missing in Los Angeles—peace, quiet, natural beauty; wild blueberries, church bells, waving neighbors, poets; salty air and millions of stars. I'd had no idea how much I missed the East Coast, and a happiness flooded my body. New house next to me or not, I was in love, and my love for that beautiful state and its people grows stronger with every moment I spend there. What Disney World is to kids, Maine is to me. L.A. may be where I flourish as a businesswoman, but Maine is where my heart wants to be.

The next day my beautiful friend Becky arrived in her high heels and short dress and began turning cartwheels on the front lawn. Uh-oh, people were going to start talking about us; I just knew it. Becky is one of the most outgoing people I know, so naturally she struck up a conversation with Mike. I think I yelled at her and told her to stay away from that house and the "workers," as I called them (how obnoxiously haughty I was), knowing that she was going to create a stir around town with her blond hair and long legs. But of course she couldn't help herself and she offered to buy the guys some beer. We went in to the local IGA and bought a six-pack of Corona Light with lime because that's what I wanted. I decided that I should be the one to deliver the beer since Becky's sexiness might distract the "workers" and, who knows, one of them could lose a finger or worse, fall off the roof. I walked over and no one was there, so I took one bottle out of the six-pack for myself and left the rest.

That evening we walked over to one of the neighbors' houses for dinner. Side Note: The hosts of that dinner, our other neighbors Bill and Susan, have since become our family. We get so excited when we turn down that long road to enter Prospect Harbor knowing we'll soon be seeing them. I get that feeling I got as a child when I was heading to see my nanny Mary and papa John. The older I get, the more I realize that you want to find modern-day versions of the people you loved and lost.

I left the party for about fifteen minutes to show someone our house and that's when I formally met Mike who was the contractor building the problematic property. He thanked me for the Coronas, which I have since discovered is the last beer on earth a guy from Maine wants to drink, especially with a twist of lime.

My first reaction was that he was hot. My second was that he sooo did not look like a contractor. Every contractor I have ever known had hair growing out of his ears and a gut. He introduced himself and was very polite. He had a ridiculously cute boyish smile and I was instantly taken but more as in "Summer Nights" from *Grease* than "Endless Love" from *Endless Love*. Maybe the almost-built house wasn't so bad after all. We spoke briefly and I headed back to dinner .

After dinner, we noticed that Mike and his coworker Sean had started a bonfire. I took it to be some sort of mating call or romantic gesture. Mike swears he was burning scrap wood, although he kept an ember from the fire that night and later had an old man in Blue Hill, Maine, create a hand-carved frame for it as a gift for me. It hangs in our house. Whatever the case, Becky and I stopped over to say hello and he just so happened to have marshmallows, chocolate, and graham crackers that his clients had left for him. So we drank beer and ate s'mores for a few hours, a far cry from the menus of swanky L.A. restaurants like Cecconi's and the Palm, but surprisingly more enjoyable. Mike very candidly talked about his daughter, Elora, whom he obviously adored, about his divorce, and then introduced me to Tinkerbell, the Chihuahua he had bought Elora but ultimately inherited. Chihuahuas I knew about. My beloved Tikki was my family and like natural Prozac to me. A kid and an ex-wife, however, were another story. (As I would soon find out, both Elora and Mike's first wife, Rebecca, are great people.)

At the end of the evening, or rather by early morning, I asked Mike and Sean if they wanted to spend the night at my house. We had two extra bedrooms and it was freezing outside. They had been sleeping in a small trailer since the house they were building did not have heat yet. Mike politely declined, but Sean said, "Hell yeah, can I take a shower?" These guys would work days on the coast without showering or sleeping and then go back to their houses ninety minutes away on the weekend. I said good night to Mike and followed Sean into my house. Within a minute of entering the kitchen, Sean was eating the entire contents of our refrigerator and falling down the staircase. He had had a few too many and I began to see this ending in a hefty lawsuit.

I went out and asked Mike to politely tell Sean to go to bed and stop roaming around drunk. He came inside and waited until Sean fell asleep. During that time we sat on the couch in the living room and talked some more. We spoke about life, love, pain, family, work—as if we were two people confessing everything to one another because we knew we would never see each other again. We weren't hiding who we were or trying to impress each other, which is usually the case when you first meet someone. We were from two different worlds, but I had never felt so close to anyone I had just met like I did to Mike. When he hugged me he felt like an anchor, and I hung on to him for dear life. I was still spinning around with men until I met him, but in that instant he grounded me physically. It felt good to just stop. I should tell you that the night we met was the ten-year anniversary of my mother's death and I swear she was playing cupid from heaven.

When he left in the morning (all we did was kiss and hug like a couple of teenagers and sleep on the couch), he wrote me a note on his business card and left it on the kitchen counter. I never read it before leaving Maine because I unwittingly threw it in my bag. As I got in the car to leave he didn't wave or say good-bye. I thought to myself, *There are jerks even in*

Maine. I was headed to Worcester, Massachusetts, where my mother was buried, to visit her grave en route to working in New York City. The whole ride there I kept thinking about him and the innocent but deep connection I thought we had. Why, then, hadn't he even bothered to wave good-bye as I drove away?

When I got to the city, I found the note he had left me. Yay!!!!!! He was a good guy after all. I immediately texted him from my posh room at the Soho Grand Hotel, where I was being put up, which was in complete contrast to woodsy Maine and him. I told him that I had just found his note and was sorry I didn't say good-bye. We started a text romance and didn't speak until about a week later. It's amazing how when you first have feelings for somebody, you turn into a crushed-out girlie girl, waiting for their responses, wondering if they'll call. No one is immune to the beginning stages of love. It turns us all into hopeful fools.

When we finally talked, he was not in the same place I was, having visited my Web site (a not so brilliant suggestion on Becky's part that night around the campfire). Seeing all the artists I had worked with left him with a different impression. He naturally assumed I was a Hollywood hipster, like Paris Hilton or Lindsay Lohan, and that I could never adapt to a more wholesome lifestyle. He told me all of this and I was offended by his hasty judgment of me. I can count on one hand the number of nightclubs I have gone to in L.A. I hate going out late and would much rather stay home and watch a movie with a good glass of wine or a cheap one for that matter. He reconsidered and agreed that he shouldn't have jumped to conclusions and we started to talk every day. We were getting to know each other more with each passing week.

At the time I was in New York taking care of a family member who was going through a depression. Mike's sister had suffered from depression, too, so it was a familiar situation for him. He listened and comforted me, and for some reason I allowed him to do just that. I was ready for someone good to come into my life. I was sick of all the drama and dysfunction in my other relationships and was open to being truly loved.

We met in Boston one weekend and that's when we both knew there was something really there. We had so much fun; an innocent fun, like the kind you had playing after school with your neighborhood friends in the street till your mom told you it was time for dinner. Something about Mike made the free spirit in me come out. That side of me usually emerged only when I was writing songs, but he pulled it out of me every day, whether we were driving, having dinner, talking on the phone, or playing with Tikki. I felt safe with him and I knew he was a man of character.

My whole life I was raised to believe I had to marry a lawyer, doctor, or the head of some huge corporation. Mike, though, was an art teacher turned contractor and a visual artist. I never in a million years imagined that my true love would come in that package. One of my best friends, Angie, is a Christian, and loves to point out that Mike was a teacher, a carpenter, and that I met him by the sea. She jokes, Could he be Jesus?

It's not easy to maintain a romance with someone in Maine when you are entrenched in your career and working fourteen-hour days, seven days a week. We dated long distance for nearly six months, during which he saw me at my worst, like the time I landed after taking the red eye having had an acid peel that made me look like I was eighty years old. Note to Reader: I have this trick I use when I date a guy I like. Most girls are putting their best foot forward. I say show them who you are at your worst, and if they stick around they'll already know what they are getting themselves into.

We decided that after months of bicoastal dating, one of us should move to see if we were headed in a serious direction. Let's just say the market for songwriters in Bangor, Maine, isn't exactly booming, so it made more sense for him to relocate to L.A. I was financially in a position to help him avoid any real hardship in the move and that allowed us both to see if we would work. If I hadn't had money I might have had to let this wonderful man go and that's why I encourage young woman to have their own financial independence. You never know when a man like Mike is going to walk into your life. Having financial flexibility enables you to act on such good fortune. Financial stress can be death to a relationship.

He packed his stuff into a trailer and headed off to Los Angeles. But when he called me from Nebraska I realized that there was no turning back and I must admit that I started having second thoughts. I hardly knew him. What if it didn't work out? I was temporarily taking him away from Elora and his job. Just in case, I got my checkbook out and started thinking of a number that might ease the disruption to his life. But, that wouldn't have worked with a man of his integrity.

He arrived a few days later with his belongings and I swear the next day they were all put away in drawers and closets and fully integrated with my things. Except for his tools. Those went into the garage, which thankfully I never ventured into. I have no idea how he acclimated so quickly but it was a good sign.

The early months of a relationship are the most important. The indications of future failure or success are usually there, but we don't look at them carefully enough because our libido is guiding us. I started to notice that Tikki's water bowl was filled up regularly; we had food in the refrigerator (on the day he moved in I had only two items—champagne and mustard—since I was a bachelorette who frequently ate out); and things around the house that were broken miraculously got fixed. I was with a man who made my life easier and was supportive of my career. That made me want to behave in strange ways, like coming home for dinner by five so he wouldn't feel lonely in a new town. Me, the workaholic, was actually taking time to be with him and putting our relationship first. This had to be love . . .

And fate, for that matter. Not knowing I would end up with a contractor, I coincidentally had purchased a new house a few months before meeting him. It was a 1923 hunting lodge that reminded me of my maternal grandparents' vacation spot in Rhode Island. There was one room with a gigantic river-rock fireplace like the one we used to have. I walked in, took one look around, and knew I had to make it mine. I always listen to my gut even when it's telling me to do something outrageous. And I am sure glad I did. It's a very rare piece of land that feels more East Coast than Los Angeles. You can see a church steeple from the back, and when the leaves are changing, I swear that I'm in New England. Somehow, when I first laid eyes on the property, I was transported into the future and could see the events that would transpire. I must have known I was going to meet Mike or why else would I have bought it? The house was a complete wreck and needed intense renovation. My history with renovation involved a bathroom and almost pulling my hair out. (Colleges should really offer students a class on practical things like how your car and house work and how to read mortgage papers.)

Mike was very excited by the property and looked at it as a built-in job during a bad economy. While we waited for permits to get started, he spent his days painting (which is his real love and gift) and we have some of these beautiful works in our home today. I call it the house that would have killed me if he hadn't come along and saved it.

He asked me to marry him eight months after we moved in together—in Mexico at the Dreams Resort in Puerta Vallarta. I was wearing smiley-face thermal underwear (the poor guy). I have terrible circulation and am always cold, even in Mexico. But he loves me even so.

We were married in July 2009 at my house in Maine on the only day of sun anyone can recall that summer. I am positive my mother had something to do with that. Mike and I planned our wedding together. I wore my mother's gown for the prereception (Vera Wang for the ceremony), and when I look at the pictures I can see her in my face and mannerisms. My mother was definitely with me that day.

We had a small wedding of only thirty-five people, which I highly recommend. I can remember speaking with every one of my guests and I even took a few minutes to look out at my family and friends at the church. I have a wonderful mental snapshot of them. (Brides, look around and take it all in. The more you can do to personally customize your wedding, the more it will mean to you. I made the gift boxes with my stepdaughter, painted the railings with her, and gave iPods that said "life is a song, sing it" as gifts. Elora also made the place-card table out of moss and rocks from the beach.) I felt proud of my husband and me. We didn't have one fight before the wedding. Shame on those Bridezillas and more shame on the idiots who marry them.

The only fight I had was, of course, with my father, and it was a minor one. The church across the street from our home, where Mike and I were married, has two narrow aisles on either side of the pews. Since I didn't bother to have a church rehearsal (I really hate those), I didn't know that my dad and I couldn't fit in the aisle together side by side. As we were walking toward the altar we were fighting about who should go first. But it's one of my favorite memories because it was so true to our relationship and it makes me laugh when I think about it.

Mike is a combination of all the people in my life that have made me happy—my parents, grandparents, brother, and best of friends. He is kind and gentle; appreciative of the little things like my mother, grandmother, and grandfather; funny and compassionate like my brother; hardworking like my father; and a great sub for my best girlfriends when they are not around. He is also hot, which helps a lot to keep the romance going, 'cause let's be honest, you've got to work on that. But most important, I like who I am when I am with him. He makes me the best version of me I have ever been and I like myself more because of what he brings out in me. He softens the hard edge in me, and when I am being annoying he knows how to point it out in a way that does not make me get aggressive or defensive. Instead he makes me laugh at myself and want to be a better person. I think the key to finding the right partner in life is not always about who they are, but about who you are when you are with them.

I thank God for all the bad relationships in my life because besides being material for some of my hit songs, they were training for how to respond when the right person did come along. Trust me, when they do, you'll know it. To quote Lionel Richie, it'll be "Easy Like Sunday Morning" instead of "Cuts Like a Knife" by Bryan Adams. And in a world that can often be grueling, having a partner who isn't is a lifesaver.

Reflections on Writing "Ain't No Other Man" with Christina Aguilera

In terms of vocal ability, it doesn't get much better than Christina Aguilera. The prospect of working with her was extremely exciting. Ron Fair, an accredited producer and record executive who signed her to her record deal at RCA, had recommended that we meet since she was looking for a songwriter to collaborate with. I went over to her home in the Hollywood Hills. She had this fabulous sunken living room with the most fantastic view of L.A. I was taken downstairs into the media room, where I sat on a big pink fluffy ottoman waiting for her with her dogs, Stinky and Chewy.

When she came down to join me, I was struck by how petite she was. Where did that voice come from? I wondered. She introduced herself and began to tell me about the record she was making. It was a throwback to many of the great early R&B/jazz artists like Etta James and Nat King Cole. Christina had a deep respect and appreciation for the music that came before her. I liked how direct and focused she was and I got a kick out of how professionally the interview was conducted. Was this the same girl from the "Dirrty" video? Definitely not. She was all grown up.

She played me some tracks she liked and asked what melodies I would put over them. I sang whatever came to mind and actually felt a bit nervous as I was definitely being put on the spot. After about twenty minutes she thanked me for coming by and said she would be in touch. *Sure you will*, the jaded part of me thought to myself. I was very impressed by her and hoped we would meet again.

A few months passed and I had almost forgotten about our meeting when I got the call to write with her on her album, *Back to Basics*. I have extremely fond memories of our writing sessions. Christina has a soft side that the world doesn't always see, similar to myself. I was flattered that I got to witness it and that she opened up to me about so many aspects of her life. To be able to help someone communicate those moments through song is what I live for.

She did everything I hated to do well. I would hear music and have an immediate melodic and lyrical response. Christina was more methodical and would go over and over the lyrics and melodies till she was certain they were right. She used different color markers to highlight issues she had with the songs. And when it came to her singing, she would sing a lick thirty times till she felt it was perfect. I could never even hear the difference between the takes. She was very thorough and around her I felt somewhat lazy.

Toward the end of the album she was not sure we had the single yet. She was in love with this DJ premier track and kept insisting it was her single. I wasn't into it at all. The beginning of the track had a sample that said "do yo thing, honey," over and over till it made you want to throw something at the speakers. If the first thirty seconds of the song made me want to do that, imagine what a full 3:30 would do. But Christina would not let up and it was my job to listen to the artist. I didn't understand why I was so resistant to her inclination. Probably because when we started writing "Ain't No Other Man," it became clear it was about her relationship with her then husband, Jordan. Her past with men seemed to be similar to mine. She had been searching for the right one, and when she found him, it completely changed her life for the better. I wasn't on the same wavelength she was. I was in the unhealthy relationship that preceded meeting my husband. Maybe I didn't want to talk about the perfect relationship because I knew I was far from it in my own life and couldn't fathom it ever happening in the future. Whatever the case, I sucked it up (as I should've from the start) and we crafted the perfect wedding song—at least my perfect wedding song. I sang it to my husband in karaoke form at our wedding. It was one of the only times in my life I couldn't have cared less if I hit all the notes or gave a great performance, because he needed to hear the lyrics. I had unknowingly written them for him.

Eleven

NO BOUNDARIES

(Let's just skip the quote, shall we?)

s far as I'm concerned, *American Idol* Season 8 might as well have been called *Survivor*. Every moment was mentally, physically, and emotionally challenging. Every old fear or insecurity about the way I looked, what I said, and who I was leaped to the forefront of my mind before each show. They could edit out all of your stupidity in the audition rounds, but when the show went live, you were on your own, baby. At one point, I almost bought Depend undergarments as the anxiety over possibly wetting myself from nerves became a regular occurrence. It was torture.

So why did a girl with extreme stage fright and

no experience being a TV personality decide to take the job? The question is more like, how could I not? Let's be honest, who turns the biggest show on television down? My whole life has been about facing my demons and overcoming my fears. If I had walked away from this opportunity, I would have regretted it, and I knew that. I had survived an eating disorder, sexual misconduct, a host of insecurities, and the music business, so I thought I was ready for the biggest shark tank in the world—television. I was about to get eaten alive.

On the day I flew to New York for the Season 8 auditions, I sat next to Adrian Grenier from *Entourage* on the plane. It was all too perfect. Here I was about to be on TV and sitting next to a major star who asked me if I was an actress. I said no but told him about joining *Idol*. I'd been keeping the secret for way too long and it sounded impressive, although I have to say he'd have been more interested if I'd known my carbon footprint for the trip. Still, the promise of celebrity began settling in, and for the first time I felt genuinely excited. *This could be really fun . . .*

But fun is hardly the word I would use to describe the rest of my trip and the first round of auditions. The best part about those few days was the hotel room. Simon Cowell always made sure we stayed in the most fabulous of places, and if our accommodations were ever anything less than five stars, we were instantly moved. When I opened the door to my suite at the Peninsula, I felt like a queen entering her palace. Then I stepped on the itinerary on the floor. As soon as I picked it up and read it, the panic began.

3:30 A.M.: Hair and makeup will arrive
5:30 A.M.: Car to pick you up and drive you to satellite interviews
6:00–12:00 A.M.: Live satellite and print interviews

Two things scared me about this. One, who was doing my hair? I had never met the person. And two, what the hell were live satellite interviews?

At 5:45 A.M. I was ushered into a small dark room and asked to put an earpiece in my ear. I would be going live to all the Fox affiliates around the country to be introduced to the major markets as the new judge on *American Idol*. There was that word again—"LIVE." I hated how it always made my hands sweat and my heart race. I was asked to look at a smiley face on a Post-it note and pretend that it was the person I was addressing. My name was absolutely butchered by every newscaster and nobody knew anything about me or what I had done to even be considered for this position. It was like *American Idol* had plucked some random girl off the street and threw her on the show. Not only that, but my first interviews were so uncomfortable it was painfully obvious that I was not used to being in front of the camera.

Next came the print interviews for another couple of hours. Finally, after six full hours of stumbling through press, I was given a two-hour break and was told I would be going to Chelsea Piers at 3 P.M. to start auditions. WHAAAAAAT? I still had to do the auditions! My head was spinning and I hadn't even gotten to the most important part of the day—meeting my fellow judges and the contestants.

Simon, Paula, and Randy were flown in by a helicopter and greeted me at Chelsea Piers. I saw Paula first and she gave me a huge hug. It felt genuine, like, "If they were gonna screw me like this at least it was with someone I knew and liked." On camera she smiled and warmly welcomed me, but later I would get the real story about how she felt. She was rightfully upset that they hadn't told her about me until the day before the New York City auditions. I should have had the courage to call her and Randy, and for that I am sorry. Truth is, I didn't want to lose the gig.

Just around that time the picture that will haunt me for the rest of my life was taken. What kryptonite is to Superman, this picture is to me. *Who in the world is that woman and what the hell is she wearing?* Is it Peg Bundy from *Married with Children*? Teresa from *The Real Housewives of New Jersey*? Oh, shit, no: *it's me* (see the picture in the photo insert of this book). I have never seen my hair like that and the outfit was horrendous. Had I not taken a moment to look in the mirror before appearing in front of 25 million Americans? The makeup and hair were twelve hours old by that time, and man, it looked it. I resembled the drag queen version of myself. To this day

I will not wear anything with leopard print, although I did keep the top to remind myself how perilous the wrong look can be.

I didn't have much experience with creating a fashion style for myself. Nor did I have a clear sense of what I wanted to look like on television, which, I am sure, drove my hair and makeup team nuts. My off-camera style was simple—jeans, a plain shirt, and minimal makeup, but that wasn't going to work on *American Idol*. I arrived in New York with only a carry-on bag. Boy, did I get a shock when I walked into Paula's room and saw twenty pairs of shoes all beautifully lined up, stunning color-coordinated clothes everywhere, and a stylist to help with her wardrobe. There is an art to being a celebrity and having a personal style. Everything was meticulously hung up and pressed. I felt embarrassed that my clothes were still in my rolling bag and that I usually steamed them when they were already on my body.

Dressing with style takes time, effort, and vision. I, sadly, had none of that. I had a publishing company, an A&R job at Warner Bros., and a songwriting/producing career to maintain on top of my responsibilities for *Idol*, which at the time, I had no idea would be so labor intensive. Simon Cowell was smart to come up with his uniform of the white tee. It gave him more time to spend on his TV shows and business ventures. It took me until the middle of Season 9 to begin liking what I saw on TV (although I really don't look like myself with television makeup on). I was literally learning as I went and the New York auditions and subsequent pictures were evidence that I was clueless. (Thank God Mezghan Hussainy was there to be my makeup stylist/therapist.)

I was asked to sign autographs upon my arrival at Chelsea Piers. That was a truly bizarre experience. Fans of *American Idol* had not so flattering pictures of me from old music industry events a few years prior that I never in a million years thought would resurface. I wonder, *Should I sign on my face? Across my boobs? Writing my whole name would take hours, should I abbreviate it?* The fans were like "Lady, just sign it already." Later on I would come to love signing autographs. To be able to make someone smile just by writing your name on a piece of paper is the best!

After taking in all the cheering crowds who turned out to welcome the judges to New York City, we walked onto the set and I got my first dose of TV-show reality. There were easily fifty unfamiliar faces all staring at me trying to figure out who I was and what I could possibly be bringing to the show other than my big hair. These were the crew members, the behind-the-scenes people who dedicate their lives to making *Idol* the success that it is. They hadn't even heard about me until the morning of the auditions. They had to relight the whole table and scramble for an extra chair. I was the worst kind of change you can imagine. Unexpected, unnecessary, and seemingly unfabulous.

I wanted desperately to fit in on the panel. That resulted in my talking way too much and interrupting the other judges. I couldn't understand their rhythms and cues. They were a family and had been together for years. I had to catch up, learn their lingo, and figure out how to bring something unique to the show. It was painfully apparent in the beginning that I wasn't doing that. What I didn't know yet is that I needed to define a role of my own on the panel—one the others hadn't already taken. The problem was I had made a career out of being many things to many people and picking just one felt wrong and dishonest.

Randy was always kind and sweet to me. In fact, I nicknamed him "Thank God for Randy Jackson." He held my hand when we walked out on the stage at the beginning of the live shows in Season 8 and he was always encouraging. He was a good positive force for everyone he came in contact with. And while Paula took me under her wing at the early auditions, the key to gelling with the panel was Simon. I smoked way too many cigarettes (a nasty habit I had previously kicked) outside the set in an attempt to bond with him, but he just wasn't having any of it. I hated myself for seeking his approval. I have never been that person. I say what I feel and I don't kiss ass for anything, but if I couldn't get him to acknowledge and engage me, I was going to be in big trouble when that little light turned red. What was so puzzling to me was that Simon had seemed to really like me when I met him in London, so why the cold shoulder now? Something was definitely going on. And when I dared to disagree with him, the vibe was even colder.

Lunch was always a good opportunity to bond. Randy, Ryan (who was very nice and the hardest-working man I know), and Simon were the popular kids. They were the "in" clique and of course Simon was the gang leader (well he did have the private plane they all flew in). I loved listening to them. They were very funny together and spoke of their trips to Miami, their business dealings and, of course, their new toys, namely houses, all the things that fill them, and in Simon's case, cars. Simon and Ryan played a hilarious game where they would identify the most powerful person they knew in Hollywood and call their office at the same time. Whoever got them on the line first won. It went something like this:

"Hello, it's Ryan for Rupert." (I'm talking about Rupert Murdoch here, the Chairman and CEO of News Corporation, Fox's parent company.)

"Hello, it's Simon for Rupert,"

Then we would wait to see who Rupert picked up for and who was told that Rupert would call them back . . .

DRUMROLL. The winner was . . . on second thought, I think I'll leave you guessing. These men all have a lot of shows I'd like to appear on.

Anyway, I was just happy that they let me sit with them until one day I screwed up even that. I had ordered king crab claws and corn and was thoroughly enjoying my meal because it so reminded me of summers on the coast of Rhode Island during my childhood. It was my version of comfort food. When I looked up Simon was staring at me with an utterly disgusted grimace on his face. "Kahra, my God, what are you eating?" he asked. "Uh, crab, it's delicious," I replied with a half-full mouth. "Want some?" I probably had corn stuck between my teeth when I said it and my hands were no doubt soaking wet from pulling apart the poor crustacean that was my meal. He looked like he was going to throw up. I think he even left the table. I was an alien to him. Well let's be real, to everyone.

To their credit, the judges only hazed me once. I was all too eager to play a word game they had thought of a few seasons back in which they would give each other a phrase that had to be used in the context of judging a contestant. Randy gave me "buck wild mango." I went first at the next audition, and of course I excitedly incorporated the words into my critique. The producers were puzzled, like "What did she just say?" Simon, Randy, and Paula naturally did not use their phrases so I looked like a loon. I thought it was funny, though, and I was happy to see they thought I was worth playing a joke on. It was progress . . . of sorts.

The only advice and feedback I got were "Shorter comments" and "Don't interrupt King Simon." No one ever really explained the nuts and bolts of the show in a way that was helpful. If you need proof, check out YouTube and watch the live shows during Season 8 as I leaned into the microphones in front of us whenever I offered my critiques. Too bad I didn't know at the time that they were only props.

The one piece of constructive advice I received was from a British man consulting on the show whom I called "the Reaper" because I knew when he was headed my way, it was bad news. He would always say "more humanity," and he was right. My on-camera presence was cold. But that was because I felt so uncomfortable, insecure, and nervous. That woman I used to be—the one who had forged ahead in a sea of doubt and had still risen to the top of the music business despite the bumps on the road—was gone. I was in a foreign place, speaking a foreign language with no translator. I could never seem to let the real me out. Even Paula turned to me at one point and said, "Who are you? This is not the no-nonsense, ballsy, outspoken girl I know." She was right, but how could I have been that? There was already an alpha dog barking the truth and I don't think America would have appreciated it from the new judge, too. And the more I didn't fit in the more I just shut down. I was convinced that I would warm up when I got more warmth from those around me. I felt like a dinner guest who got cut from the list, but who still received the invite because of an idiot assistant's mistake. When they said reality TV, in my case they meant it. No coaching whatsoever. Just jump in and figure it out.

It took me way too long to realize that what I had signed on for was a TV show not a music show. I was expected to be a character not a music teacher or industry insider who used words like "artistry." Wow, was I ridiculed for that! God forbid we encouraged these kids to be more than just singers. All they wanted was thirty-second, snappy sound bites from me delivered with oomph! I'm part Italian and we Italians LOVE to talk. I don't think I can even say my name in less than thirty seconds. They also wanted a quick thinker. But I've always been one to take my time with artists, to get a real feel for who they are and see the range of their music abilities before I give my opinion. I often used my voice to demonstrate where a vocal went right or wrong. But Simon made it perfectly clear to me that my singing wasn't going to fly when he joked, "Ah, Kahra, Katrina [aka Bikini Girl] is way better than you." So the biggest thing I had going for me—my ability to mentor, sometimes with my own voice as example—was, in effect, banned from use. Man, I was in trouble.

I had barely survived the auditions when I heard the rumors that I had almost been axed. I was supposed to be the person mixing things up on the panel. Instead, I was messing them up. I pretty much underwhelmed everyone. I'm not delusional. I could certainly understand how annoying it must have been for all of them, especially Cowell, to have to train someone whom they thought would just innately know what to do (although I bet if you were to go back to his first shows on TV, they weren't perfect either). But it still felt like there was something more going on with him.

What I wasn't privy to at that time was that I had landed smack in the middle of a high-stakes chess game. I suspect that they hired me for many reasons, the least of which was my accomplishments in the music business. It seems to me that Fox and Freemantle, the British production company, wanted to keep Paula in check, since her contract was up in a year; Cowell wanted a fourth judge to create a new chemistry, since he felt things were getting predictable; and Simon Fuller wanted someone to stand up to Simon Cowell more.

Number one, they should have paid Paula what she wanted. She deserved it. The woman helped put the show on the map and the relationship between her and Cowell was one of the highlights of the program. And two, while it made perfect sense to me that Fuller might not want any one person to hold so much power on the panel, how could I go after Cowell? At times he may have been a pain in my ass, but he was brilliant. His comments were always spot on and he quickly became one of the most interesting people to hit TV in years. That's why he emerged as the star of the show and one of most respected men in the music business.

My sad take is that they were never interested in me for my accomplishments or how I could really help the contestants. As proof of that . . . I don't think I was ever properly credited or introduced to the viewers. It felt more like I was there to serve ulterior motives and ones that I could never achieve for them. I'm willing to bet that in Simon Cowell's mind, I was Simon Fuller's girl, and that made me suspect no matter what I said and did. Under those circumstances, I could see why Cowell was less than kind to me at times, but it still hurt.

The landscape became even more complex when the show went live and I was reviewed by the American public. I was crucified. The biggest mistake I ever made was checking out the blogs to see what everyone thought of me. "Idiot, moron, horrid, butta face" were the usual words associated with my name." (The last term, BTW, means that everything "but her face" is attractive—in case, like me, you didn't know.) I had never in my life heard such things said about me. I was at the top of my game in the music business after years of fighting to get there. But as far as television was concerned, I might as well have been Sinéad O'Connor after she ripped up a picture of the pope. Persona non grata.

All that "love" spilled over into the live shows when Ryan introduced the judges . . .

Ryan: "Let me welcome Randy Jackson." People would be screaming, crying, lighting themselves on fire . . . "DAWG, DAWG."

"And Kara DioGuardi . . ." Crickets . . . I was mortified. I started clapping for myself just to cover up the silence.

"And Paula Abdul . . ." The fans went nuts again and the cheering roared to an all-time high.

"And last but not least, SIMON Cowell." I literally could not hear at that point; the clapping was deafening.

I wanted to DIE.

In hindsight, I realize that I was relying on a tactic that had gotten me through my first days of working with Enrique Iglesias on the *Escape* record. I was acting "as if" I had an expertise until I actually acquired it . . . but acquiring the expertise to be a television judge before millions of viewers was a very different situation. I should have just leveled with everyone and laughed at my own mistakes, instead of tensing up and trying so hard to cover them up or not make them at all. Perhaps that was what was meant by the encouragement I received to show "more humanity." I needed to be a bit more humane to myself.

The critics also nailed me to the cross. They picked up every stupid thing I did wrong, like when I mistakenly said I would rather have heard Danny Gokey singing something from older Aerosmith material when what I really meant to say was from Aerosmith's newer songs. (He had sung "Dream On.") They were unmerciful. Of course I knew I made a mistake but there was no way to correct it as they had already moved on to Paula. Every slip of the tongue or awkward gesture I made was blown out of proportion. Hadn't anyone heard my other comments, or listened between the lines to notice me genuinely trying to give these kids constructive musical advice, not just advice on presentation?

At times it felt like no one in the press cut me a break. But one of them did make nice drawings on my face. I remember the first lovely penis that Perez Hilton drew across my photo (he actually draws decently). He was briefly aligned with Warner Bros., where I worked, and even after he made his negative opinion of me on *Idol* known in his blog, I still met with him and tried to help him navigate the music industry by giving him names of producers who could possibly help to develop his artists at the time. When asked by my then-boss, Tom Whalley, what I thought of Perez's acts, I gave my true opinion, since that is what I was paid to do. I believe he really showed his lack of musical knowledge when he said that Travis Garland was a better talent and singer than Justin Timberlake. Anyone who was even considering hiring him had to rethink their decision after that comment.

When Tom left Warner, Perez sent me an e-mail that same day. Even though the subject line read "Hey Sweetie," there was nothing about the content that was endearing. He wanted me to know that he had ears *everywhere* and was very aware that I shared my opinions of his roster with the higher-ups at Warner. But the sweetest part of all is when he promised to repay my kindness TENFOLD. That's right, he wrote it in caps, topped it off with an exclamation point, then added "Mark my words!" before signing it with the universal symbols for hugs and kisses, but somehow all those xs and os felt very, very menacing to me. As did his timing. Did he think that with the changing of the guard my position at Warner Bros. would be adversely effected? Was he gloating over my supposed vulnerability? I don't know, you tell me. I will add, though, that he subsequently tweeted about me asking if I was okay, which I took to mean that he thought I wasn't. This is all to say that you can't always believe what you read about people. One never knows the real story or the possible complex motivations of the snarky character assassinations committed online every day. And in the case of Perez, I think it's sad that the public gives so much power to someone who relishes the negative.

I did thankfully manage to sway my Season 8 nemesis, *Entertainment Weekly*'s Michael Slezak, in Season 9 and at least his insults were well written, intelligent, and humorous.

But, even when there was good press, something always went wrong. I got into *People*'s "100 Most Beautiful" issue, which was an unbelievable feeling. Not because I think that I am a great beauty (believe me, I don't), but because it was surreal to be in a group with people like Angelina Jolie and Halle Berry.

But then I read my quote. They had asked me what my routine consisted of when getting ready for a show. Since a music executive had once told me I needed a nose job, I have always been insecure about that part of my face, so I used to ask my makeup artist to shade the sides of it to make it look smaller. Well, the quote read, "I like to shave my nose before a show." *Great, now everyone thinks I have nose hair.*

The torture of Season 8 escalated to an all-time high when Charles Boyd, one of the most supportive producers, came to me a few weeks before the finale with an idea. He wanted to invite Bikini Girl back to sing "Vision of Love." He thought it would be hilarious if she would come out onstage in her bikini and begin singing the song, then at some point they would turn her microphone down and I would surprise her from behind completing the chorus. At the end of the performance I'd rip my dress open to reveal my own bikini. I laughed my ass off when I heard the idea but then realized what Charles had said. *Me* singing in front of 30 million people? Could I take a Valium before going on, and I'm sorry . . . did I hear something about a bikini? I told Charles it was a brilliant idea but NO FREAKING WAY! Taking my clothes off and duping some girl on television wasn't me. And that's probably why everyone loved it, especially Simon.

Simon: Kahra, I heard what you are going to do and I think it's brilliant.

Kara: What am I doing?

Simon: You know, the bikini bit.

Kara: Oh yeah. I'm not doing that.

Simon: Kahra, you must do it, it's hilarious and the audience will LOVE it.

Kara: There is no way I am going to get into a bikini on live TV.

Simon: I'm telling you, you must do it. You take yourself way too seriously.

Well, someone on the show had to and Simon was starting to sound like my dad coaxing me to sing at my grandpa's eightieth birthday party.

Simon: Promise me you will do it. Let's shake on it.

Kara: No way.

Simon: C'mon, shake. Now.

Of course, this was during a break and two minutes before going live and God knows what Simon would have done if I didn't agree. I imagined more rolling of the eyes and making "why did we ever hire you?" faces, so I said yes and shook his hand. But I never had any intention of doing the skit.

A few weeks went by and I heard nothing more about it, until one day there was a knock on my dressing-room door.

Producer: So, Kahra [everyone was British on this show], we need
      to speak about wardrobe for the skit.
Kara: What wardrobe? I'm not doing it.
Producer: C'mon. Let's at least get the wardrobe ready so if you
      decide to do it, it's there.
Kara: There is no way.

I tried to explain to them that I was a woman who thought you should lead with your brains not your body and that doing otherwise went against everything I stood for. Everyone from my team was adamant about me not doing it. They were worried about my credibility. It escalated to a point where Simon Fuller and all the producers from Freemantle and the executives from Fox brought me into a room where they passionately pleaded, arguing that it would be a great TV moment, which was only further proof that I was there more for the purpose of entertainment and less for my expertise in music. And while I could be entertaining under the right circumstances, let's be honest, I definitely wasn't moving the laugh-o-meter.

I left the meeting in a state of terror. What was I going to do? I wasn't trying to be a diva. I truly wanted to be cooperative, but what they were asking me to do seemed above and beyond the call of duty. I couldn't sleep or eat. It was one week to finale and everybody was going to be very disappointed if I didn't do the segment. I knew it would be funny but I was scared out of my mind about what could go wrong and didn't feel good about embarrassing Katrina (aka Bikini Girl) on television. What if she hit me? Or worse, started crying?

The day before the finale I still hadn't committed to doing the skit. They asked me to rehearse in case I changed my mind. Katrina was not there so my practice round consisted of going through the motions, and ripping off my dress at the end. The producers and network executives waited with baited breath for the big bikini-baring moment. I opened my dress, and that was it. They were all over me, most likely because, as a result of all the stress the situation was causing me, I had lost that layer of fat that kept my ab muscles hidden. "You *have* to do this," they all said.

I only green-lighted it the day of the finale after they promised they would give me money to build a recording studio at another Phoenix House facility and publicly announce that on the show. If I was going to make an ass of myself, at least it would be for a good cause. I have a feeling Simon told them that a charitable contribution would sway me since once he asked me if I would dye my hair blond for a show and I said "only if you give me money for a charity." He replied "How about teaching dogs to talk?" Obviously, I wasn't going to dye my hair for that but Simon suspected I might strip down for a donation to a non-profit organization of my choice.

I was so busy freaking out over the bikini skit that I had forgotten all about the other important event that was happening during that show. I had cowritten the winner's song. This had been troublesome from the start. Simon Fuller had suggested I involve Cathy Dennis, a brilliant songwriter signed to 19 Entertainment whose credits included "Toxic" by Britney Spears and "I Kissed a Girl" by Katy Perry. I was very excited to work with her, but we were both headstrong writers who didn't always see eye to eye during the writing process. The song may have suffered because of that. Additionally, I was not feeling much like a winner those days and writing "a winner's song" per se is a difficult task. Efforts to do so usually come off as trite because it's a contrived situation and songs that result from forced scenarios don't always come from an honest place. This song was also more suited for a female and that negatively affected Kris Allen and Adam Lambert's performances. Watching them sing that live was like watching a plane fall from the sky. You just wanted it to be over. When I saw Cathy in the hallway that night, she must have felt the same way because she laughed and joked, "Please don't tell anyone I wrote that." No worries, I'd take the blame for another disastrous moment on the show. There were so many already, adding another to the pile couldn't make it any worse. One of my greatest areas of expertise—writing songs—was now under scrutiny. Were there no boundaries to the hell I would endure on this show?

So between the embarrassment of the winner's song and everything else that had gone wrong during the season, the finale was starting to feel like a finale for me—I felt as if I was done, as if this was my last hoorah, my final curtain call . . . and in some ways I was hoping it was.

But all of that magically disappeared when I flashed my bikini. Here I was, a woman who, all of her life, had prided herself on her talent and her business savvy. Who would have thought that my body (which I had struggled with for so many years) would be the very thing that would convince America to give me a second chance? I can't remember the skit or even performing the song. But when it was over, it was like someone had told me that I didn't have cancer after all. I was not gonna die. I had faced two of my greatest fears that night . . . singing in front of people (in this case tens of millions!) and baring my body in public. It was like I had won the Olympics. I felt badly for Bikini Girl, but in truth, we had really helped each other out. She had her moment in the spotlight and I got to show America that I did have a sense of humor. When we see each other out now we always say hello. I know the experience was ultimately a good thing for both of us. Simon Cowell and the show's executives had been right!

When we wrapped, I went back to my trailer outside the Nokia Theatre and bawled uncontrollably for twenty minutes. I had been walking on eggshells for months, having no control over anything and unable to just let go. The sorrow poured out of me. I had gone from the heights of success to the depths of humiliation . . . and there was something very familiar about that. Although I had experienced highs and lows before, none were ever quite this public. The good news was that I had survived. The warrior that I had become the day my mother died was back and she was armed with her indomitable fighting spirit. There would be no more feeling sorry for myself. Season 9 would be a breeze now.

Except that it wasn't. It started on a low note when I was shocked to learn that Paula had left the show. I couldn't believe it. She was the heart of the panel, and I never thought I'd see an *American Idol* without her. Me, Simon, and Randy . . . how the hell was that going to work? The good news was that I had a year under my belt. I had been through the boot camp and brutalization of Season 8 and I felt more confident. I didn't care as much about what people thought anymore. I was gaining my strength back. I was a married woman by this time and I knew all I really needed was my husband, family and friends so if my television career went south I'd still survive the fall. My perspective had changed, and with it my attitude.

Thankfully, Simon only singled me out once in Boston, and this time I hadn't really done anything to deserve it and everyone knew it. He stopped the auditions in mid-taping and said he wanted a break. Victoria Beckham (who was guest judging) thought she had done something wrong. We went over to him to find out what was going on. "No, Victoria, it's not you, it's Kahra . . . she's talking too much." He railed on a bit more about me after that.

Now, I always admitted when I was a blabbermouth, but this time it was me and Randy who were both laughing and joking around. Simon wouldn't go after his cohort, of course, so he blamed me instead.

Victoria was so shocked by the way he spoke to me that she must have told her manager, Simon Fuller, about it because the very next day my agent called to see how I was feeling. I was thankful to Victoria for finally clueing someone in to the antics I had to endure but by this time I was fine. I had a new perspective on Simon. I wasn't going to tiptoe around him. If he spoke to me, cool; if he didn't it was his problem. I was there to do a job and that's what I was going to do until they got rid of me. No more pleasing anyone. This season I wanted to look in the mirror without throwing up. This season I was determined to be truer to myself. The less I cared about what others thought the more comfortable I became, as that had always been my signature style before. I was known for speaking my mind and being a straight-shooter off the show and was determined to be that person in Season 9. The more at ease I was, the more I could listen to the contestants and give constructive feedback. I was finally starting to hit my stride, and it felt good.

I learned that Ellen DeGeneres was going to be the new judge through the Internet while I was on a flight back from New York. The producers and execs at Fox had tried calling me earlier but didn't get through to me until I was already in the air. I was very excited to learn the news. I was a big fan of Ellen's and still am.

Meeting her and Portia was definitely a celebrity moment. They invited my husband and me over for dinner. They had a beautiful, Zen-like home. When you walk in you immediately felt calmer and more at peace. You definitely need a retreat like that when you are as busy as Ellen.

We spoke about *Idol* and I shared with her the challenges that I had gone through during Season 8. Of course, her experience would be totally different, as she was a superstar and a seasoned veteran of television. She was a huge fan of the show and seemed excited, but understandably nervous. Music or no music background, the job was not as easy as everyone thought.

After discussing *Idol*, we moved on to other subjects and the wine continued to flow. This was not at all like the everyday bottles of wine that I buy. It was more like a hundred-bucks-a-sip vintage and it tasted like liquid candy. We were having so much fun, talking and drinking. And then I asked, "You got any cigarettes?" Ellen said they didn't smoke, but I couldn't leave the poor woman alone. "C'mon. I know someone's gotta have a pack around here somewhere." It was like some alien had taken over my body. My husband was mortified. I'd turned into a drunk, chain-smoking fool before his very eyes. I think I even relit a butt. And then came the first pang of nausea. I looked up at Ellen as she was speaking and I thought *I am going to throw up on her*. This would not be a good first impression so I went to the place I always go when I am about to laugh nervously or react inappropriately—to a picture of Jesus on the cross in the attic at my first house on Baraud Road in Scarsdale, New York. I don't consider myself a Catholic anymore, but something about that picture puts me back on the straight and narrow. I went home that night and puked my guts out. I'm sure Ellen thought I was certifiable.

We met again during Hollywood week. We laughed about that night as we waited for Simon to arrive. We might have been the only ones smiling at that point because Simon just announced he was leaving the show after 9 seasons. The combination of his exit and tardiness was not a great welcome for her and when we reconvened for the live shows the following February I ended up sitting next to him—which seemed like both a promotion and a punishment at the same time.

We lost some really good talent during Hollywood week. One loss in particular took us by surprise. This contestant was in the pile with all the other contestants the judges wanted to keep when we met with the producers, but for some reason I saw her walking down the aisle of the auditorium crying and realized that she had been cut. We thought it was an oversight. She was still on the judges' list. So Randy, Ellen, Simon, and I tried to fight for her, but we weren't permitted to change the decision. There was one other contestant some of us wanted as well, but there seemed to be an air of suspicion that Simon might be trying to sabotage the contestant pool in the wake of his leaving. I don't know about that, but from my perspective he was definitely trying to help the show. I felt awful for these contestants. I wanted to go in and cut a song with one of them, but contractually we were not supposed to speak to them for a predetermined period of time. By the end of the week I didn't have a good feeling about the mix of talent we'd ended up with, and I was right.

When people ask what happened to the talent in Season 9, I give them my opinion plain and simple: the guest judges' ability to vote negatively in some instances impacted the contestant pool in Hollywood. Simon's vote was usually a no (that was his role), which left me and Randy most times saying yes and if the guest aligned with Simon, we'd lose them as Simon's vote was the tie breaker. This is where not having Paula really hurt the show. She probably would have aligned with me and Randy, and we would have had more people going through to Hollywood for a second chance and second chances are critical. People screw up and get nervous. You have to be able to see through that and give them another go.

When we first went live the contestants really blew it. At one point, I used the word "depressing" to describe the atmosphere. I got in trouble for that. The producers and execs were always encouraging me to say things that were more positive. The most important message needed to be that the talent was great. But if I started my comments with something upbeat and followed with suggestions as to what the contestants could have done better the producers felt that I ended on a low note. I felt as if they were never satisfied. They would urge me to reverse the pattern, but I just couldn't get my head around how to start with a negative and end with a positive, and I had my credibility to think of. After years of viewing *Idol*, it seemed to me that the American public was educated enough to know when something is great and when it's not. So I turned my focus to praising those contestants who deserved it and actually helping the others see where they could have done better and where their performances fell flat. I must say that after every episode I still wanted to rush the stage and whisper in each contestant's ears what more they needed to improve upon and what songs they should be singing. The fact that I could not mentor them was the most frustrating part of *Idol*.

I also found that going third in the judging was much easier than going second. During Season 8, when I followed Randy, I had never wanted to disagree with him because I loved him and he was so supportive of me. He also did a great job of getting the crowd riled up. Being critical right after him would have brought everyone down. And by the way, it was not fun to be booed by the crowd. But during Season 9 going third meant that I was speaking right before Simon, which made it possible for me to point out the shortcomings of the contestants. I'm pretty sure he was going to go there anyway.

Soon Simon started to agree with me. What had happened? Why now? I think he realized that I knew what I was talking about. It wasn't the greatest dynamic for him, as he would have much preferred to contradict me, but I could tell he was having fun when he would whisper in my ear all the critiques he thought I should offer later, especially when Katie Stevens was singing. He felt she was country and I thought she was pop with a soul twist. He told me there was a new genre called "Suntry," which was a combination of soul and country, and that I should encourage her to look into that style of singing in my comments. He almost had me believing in this fictitious genre. Of course I didn't fall for it, but I laughed my ass off at how he had concocted this whole thing to make me look stupid. I was dealing with the biggest jokester known to mankind, and not only did he see that I appreciated his humor, but I think he noticed that I wasn't taking it all too seriously anymore.

There was also that time that Big Mike sang "A Woman's Worth." At the time I was on my second round of IVF treatments and full of fertility drugs. I absolutely loved Mike's performance and that song, but I think the drugs impacted my emotions and I began to tear up. Simon could have embarrassed me but he didn't. Instead he put his arm around me. The ice was starting to melt.

I think Simon also started to see me as someone who thought for herself and was nobody's tool. He started to respect me. And even though he had been hard on me in the beginning, I suspect he had always known I had a lot to offer. Deep down, I'd always known he was incredible at what he does. He wasn't just a judge on *American Idol*. He was producing as he went along. His analogies and opinions were the kind that everyone could understand. He taught me more about television in two years than I could have ever learned in twenty, even if just by osmosis. He pushed my buttons to see what I was made of and showed me how strong I really was. So the man I hated in Season 8 was the man I actually cried for on the last day of Season 9, when he said his good-bye and out of everyone, I felt I grew the most because of him.

I remember the moment when I knew *I* wouldn't be back. I just had a sense—that momentary glimpse into the future you sometimes get. A premonition really. I looked up as the confetti came down on Lee DeWyze after he sang his final song. I turned to my right and saw Ellen DeGeneres and then turned to my left and saw Simon Cowell, and thought this is why I tortured myself and did everything I was scared of. Look at the icons I was standing next to. How the hell did I get here? And what if this is one of the biggest moments of my life? In that one second I gave thanks for the incredible ride I had been on with *Idol*, and for its family, no matter how bumpy our journey together had been.

I had no idea that Ellen was leaving the show after Season 9 and was shocked to hear news about the show through the Internet again. When it came to decision making at *Idol*, I thought I had been in the loop. I definitely was not. As far as I knew and had been told, the show was only looking for a replacement for Cowell. I was even more confused when I read articles about my alleged firing that fateful day during my summer vacation in Maine. I had just spoken to one of the producers a couple of weeks prior about the Season 10 audition schedule. When I called to confront the show's executives about the news, they told me I was *not* fired but that Ellen's exit definitely put a new twist on things. I asked them point blank if I was going to still be on the show during Season 10. They could not with 100 percent certainty confirm that. They began throwing names around as possible additions to the panel and there was one name in particular that made it impossible for me to see myself on the show during Season 10—not because of that person, but because of some history surrounding them.

I am not one for feeling powerless. Was I going to sit on the sidelines and wait to see what would happen (which meant keeping my schedule open and possibly interfering with other aspects of my career) or was I going to bow out on my own terms? I had four other jobs, many people who relied on me, and I had already pushed events on my calendar around to accommodate the show's auditions twice. Plus, I wanted a child and there was no way I could get pregnant under the stress of eighteen-hour work days and live TV. As I mentioned before, I had undergone three unsuccessful rounds of IVF during Season 9. I decided it was time for me to leave, so my manager called the producers at Freemantle and the executives at Fox to tell them that and subsequently sent an email conveying my desire to be released from my option. That e-mail appears below.

From: "Stephen J. Finfer" ◄━━━━━━━━━━━━━━━━━━►

Date: August 5, 2010 10:41:54 PM PDT

To: Cecile Frot-Coutaz ◄━━━━━━━━━━━━━━━━━━━━━

Cc: "Jamieson Roberts, Esq." ━━━━━━━━━━━━━━━━━,

Jeff Frasco ◄━━━━━━━━━━━━━━━

Subject: Kara DioGuardi -w- FremantleMedia/American Idol

Dear Cecile:

   Further to our earlier conversation, and for all the reasons discussed, we look forward to hearing from Fremantle regarding Kara's desire to negotiate a release from her agreement with American Idol Productions. Please advise Fox accordingly, and let me know everyone's thoughts at your earliest convenience.

Thanks and regards,

Stephen

Stephen J. Finfer
ArtHouse Entertainment
━━━━━━━━━━━━━━━━━━━
━━━━━━━━━━━━━━━━━
Ph: ━━━━━━━━━
Fax: ━━━━━━━━━
Mobile: ━━━━━━━━━
check out: ━━━━━━━━━━━━

But they would not do that until they had a firm panel in place. I interpreted that to mean that I was their backup plan. Why else would they not have released me? For weeks I watched as I was speculated about in the press and no one from the show made a statement or defended me, which was hurtful. I think the producers felt they needed celebrities to fill the judges' spots. I may have become a pseudo-celebrity while there, but I didn't have millions of fans who adored me before getting the job. Most people still didn't know exactly what I do in relation to the music business anyway. On top of not being a famous name, there was also no schtick with me. I wasn't the nice one, the mean one, or the zany one, and I wasn't going to start being a character or TV personality just for the sake of staying on the show. Trust me, the character in me belonged on cable and if I'd started in, the FCC would have fined the show millions of dollars for the f-bombs I dropped. Leaving was painful and there will always be a part of me that wanted to stay. But my desire to be in control of my destiny was larger than my need to be a household name. Looking back, I wish I had wowed America from the start and been better than I was during the first season. But I am human and was in an impossible position. I did the best I could. And when you've done the best you could, you have nothing to be ashamed of.

Yesterday I was standing in a vintage furniture store when the owner said, "We won't be seeing you on *Idol* next year?" I've gotten this question a lot since my exit. He went on to say something to the effect of "you weren't crazy enough and there were no scandals surrounding you." That's right—I was too "normal" on the show. NORMAL. There's that word again. It's funny how that was all I wanted to be when I was younger. Then, of course, when I decided that I wanted to be recognized for my gift, I had to fight to be seen as different and now I wasn't seemingly outrageous enough for *Idol*. I've been wrestling with that word one way or another my whole life. But this time I was happy to be referred to as that. I walked away realizing that what he had meant to say (or rather what I was hearing) was I had not lost my moral center; I had not sold out to anyone; I hadn't engaged in a scandal just for the sake of it, and lastly I wasn't anyone's puppet. I left that store holding my head high because I realized my integrity and credibility were intact. Those are two things you can never get back once you trade them in for anything less meaningful. NO, I was a success on the show in my own right, and with that affirmation, an enormous sense of peace came over me.

Forget what everyone else thinks. This is what I think. Nothing feels better than knowing you didn't let your fears stand in your way. I went from being a young girl always seeking approval to a woman holding her own in a catch-22 situation. Whether I was great or not on *American Idol* was beside the point. I jumped in the water. And I swam. I might have felt like shark bait at times, but I took the plunge anyway, kept afloat, and guess what? I'm still alive and more ready than ever for what comes next.

Was it a helluva high note? Yes, but in the end I'm still glad I reached for it, and all the other high notes in my life. If I didn't go for those high notes I wouldn't be where I am today.

Epilogue

s I was nearly done writing this book I had a profound understanding of some things that mystified me up until this point. I wondered if I had so many moments of happiness in my life, why were the darker times more prevalent in my psyche and on the page?

The answer suddenly seems simple: my struggles are what I tapped into most often when writing songs. They are what I needed to overcome and what was on my mind in the moment. I found writing about them to be integral in dealing with my issues and hopefully some listeners found comfort in hearing the subject matter and knowing they were not alone. But you never know, maybe this newfound awareness will lead me in all kinds of different lyrical directions—don't be surprised if I reflect more on the joys of life in future songs!

Also, if you, like me, wondered why I didn't immediately rectify certain injustices in my business and personal life when they occurred, I hope the answer is now clear. On some very deep level I believed that if I had, I would never have achieved what I have or have gotten to where I am today—sharing my experiences with you. I needed to stay on my songwriting journey in order to reach my full potential and I was afraid that if I spoke out certain important doors would close. I didn't want to go into battle without knowing I could win the war. I only brought up these events now because they are an integral part of my story. But the beauty of my revelation is that I am no longer in a war with any of these people or myself for that matter, which is why I can discuss these happenings so openly. I wish that same peace for you while on your own journey of self-discovery.

—Kara DioGuardi

Prospect, Maine, December 2010

Appendix A

MY COMMANDMENTS FOR
DETERMINED SONGWRITERS

s you now know, I've had to learn a lot about the business of music on the job. Some lessons were hard learned; others were made easier by the existence of some amazing mentors. Following in these mentors' footsteps, I'd like to share what have become my personal tenets. They appear below in no particular order as they have all been the most important rule at different moments throughout my career. May they prove as useful to you as they have been to me.

Know Thyself and Come from a Place of Truth

It took me years to figure out what was buried deep inside of me. We are taught to hide our feelings because they show vulnerability which can be interpreted as weakness. Most people aren't even aware of what's going on inside them. When they hear a song it tugs on their own emotions and brings those sentiments to the surface. That's why the joy in "At Last" by Etta James can make a father cry at his daughter's wedding or the angst of "(Smells Like) Teen Spirit" can make a crowd start to shout. Your bare, uncensored emotions should fuel the song. You must communicate your truth honestly so that when the listener hears it, they can relate to it. Your sentiment should always be believable. That's why it took me so long to write a good song. I had no idea who I was or what I felt. What made me fall in love with No Doubt was when Gwen Stefani was courageous enough to bare her devastation over her breakup with bandmate Tony Kanal. Here was a superstar showing us that she is just like us, not immune to heartbreak. She wasn't a tough punk-rock chick—she was human. Find the human in your story and always come from your heart.

Keep a Journal or a Recorder Next to You at All Times

Some of the best songs out there are based on things people have said during a conversation with one of their cowriters. They are themes that are all around us in every day conversation. You may have uttered an incredible title when you were speaking with your best friend on the phone. If you have a journal with you it will train your brain to be ready for when you drop those gems. Toby Gad and BC Jean, who cowrote "If I Were a Boy" for Beyoncé, shared with me how they came up with the concept. They were in New York City walking by a pizza place and BC said, "I wish I were a boy because if I was I would eat pizza and junk food all day." Toby stopped and said, "What else would you do if you were a boy?" and the words and melodies started pouring out.

There are even times where a song will follow an event happening in real time. My friend Brian Howes, who cowrote "Lips of an Angel," said he literally took the opening lines from a phone conversation that happened while he was in the room. Every moment of your life is potential material for a great song. Be ready for it.

The same thing applies to melody lines. You may have a great melodic idea for a song, but if you have nothing to record it with, you will lose it forever. I have literally woken up in the middle of the night singing something that ultimately became a song. The chances of me getting out of bed, going downstairs, and finding a recorder are slim to none, so I keep one on my nightstand. Always run a tape when you are writing. Your first ideas may be your best, and if you are not taping them, you won't recall what your instincts were. So many of my songs were written around the very first melody or lyric that came to mind. I won't even listen to a track or someone playing an instrument without a recorder on. Songs like "Pieces of Me" and "Undo It" would not have existed without this discipline.

Practice Makes Perfect

I often sit on these music industry panels and give advice to people who want to become professional songwriters. I always ask them how much time they spend writing songs. When they tell me they try and write once or twice a week, I tell them that music is their hobby. If you are not writing every day, then you are not serious about this as an occupation. At the height of my success I was writing two songs a day.

It's like a sales job; the more you cold call the better your chances of making a sale. The more songs you write the likelier you are to land a big one. I wrote hundreds of songs before I wrote my first hit and they were all important in getting me to that place. With each one I learned the art of songwriting until one day everything came together in the form of a big song.

Don't get stuck on one song for a month. Keep writing. You may look back after writing a few others and figure out you didn't like the one that stumped you after all, or you may figure out exactly what needed to be done to complete it. The only way to get better as a songwriter is to write, write,

write. When I get back from a vacation it usually takes me a few songs before I come up with anything good. It's like a muscle that atrophies if you don't work out. The more you use your writing muscles the stronger they become.

Find Your Champion

Every creative person needs someone who they can download to. Entering the music business feels like an insurmountable challenge. Find a person who can be your sounding board and keep you focused when you want to give up or when you are stumbling through a song with potential and have lost your way. I've had three champions who were instrumental in my career: Joe Lodi, who told me I was talented and should keep going; Clyde Lieberman, who helped me get to the right people and stay focused; and my now partner/manager Stephen Finfer, who helps me maximize my career financially while keeping me away from the ledge. This person should comfort you when you are having a bad day but encourage you to write. When you are so close to something, it's often hard to see the big picture. This person will remind you of that. Without them, it's a lonely road.

There Is No Good Anymore, Just Great

When I was coming up, a songwriter could have album cuts and make a good living. The market has become singles driven so artists are not looking for good songs, they are looking for hit singles. This has made being a songwriter more competitive than ever. Sometimes it takes a combination of people to write a hit song. If you look at most of the hit songs out there today, there are many writers listed. Don't be afraid to involve other writers in the process. Someone's ideas on what you have written so far could be the difference between a good song and a great song, and 100 percent of something mediocre is worth nothing.

Team Up with Producers

You want to be creating as close to master-quality records as you can. Record executives cannot hear through one instrument demos. Country is the only market that can still get a guitar vocal, and even that's changing. Working with producers will guarantee that your songs sound marketable as they are the ones who are responsible for the current trends and soundscapes on the radio. Don't concentrate solely on getting your songs to labels, as the producers in most cases control albums' creative content alongside the artists. The goal is to use your songwriting skills to meet producers who need you to write on their tracks and for their projects. If you can't get to any established producers, then find ones who show promise and have a unique sound (there is more about that in "Be Proactive"). I owe most of my success to the fact that I was always working with a great producer who was getting a lot of work that flowed over to me. I used my voice as leverage because I could actually sing what I was hearing in my head, and at the end of the day we had high-quality demos that once the artist vocaled, with a few tweaks became records. If you can't sing, make sure you team up with someone who can interpret your ideas and bring the song to life.

Be Proactive

If you think that you will get noticed by sitting in your apartment writing songs in a vacuum, you're on the wrong path. You need to get out there and have your name circulating. Use the Internet to post your music and connect with other writers and producers on sites like MySpace. Make a list of writers/producers that have inspired you and write to their Web sites. Some of them will have internships available so you can do some side work for them and in return maybe they'll listen to your music. Be resourceful. My shining-star creative executive at Arthouse, Katy Wolaver, was hired from an e-mail she sent to my site, and my lifesaving assistant Cristi Vaughan through Facebook. Sign up with a performing rights society (BMI, ASCAP, SESAC) and participate in their songwriting workshops so you can meet other writers and producers in your situation and begin creating a community. Offer yourself up as an unpaid intern at any of the performing rights organizations, recording studios, music magazines, record labels, production companies, or management companies. Whenever you are around the music business you will be learning skills you can use in the future whether on the creative or business side. Many people got their start this way. If I hadn't taken that assistant position at *Billboard*, who knows where I would be. And if you are an aspiring artist, play everywhere you can as often as you can and always keep a CD close by. You never know who may be in the audience.

Pitching Songs Is Hard. Develop Artists.

It's very rare now that an artist records a song they haven't cowritten. Publishing is one of the greatest sources of income and most artists, rightly so, want a piece of it. The chances as an aspiring writer that you will be able to get your song recorded by Katy Perry or get in the room with her are very slim. Too many times young writers are solely concentrating on creating songs for current artists. They often use the songs these artists have out at the time as templates and end up writing derivative compositions with soon-to-be-outdated productions. You have to remember that the songs you hear on the radio were written months before they came out. Chances are Katy Perry's next record won't sound anything like her present one.

The market changes quickly. In order to maximize your chances of getting a song published, you should think of helping to develop new, unsigned talent. Jason Reeves and Colbie Caillat collaborated together on songs for her way before she was signed to Universal Republic. She and Jason cowrote "Bubbly," which became an international hit and launched both their careers. They weren't worrying about what Ke$ha or Train were doing.

They concentrated on developing their own thing and making it unique to the marketplace. Find artists out there that need music for their projects. Use the Internet to scout them. You'll have a built-in home for your songs once the artists release their albums. Songwriters are now part of the new artists and repertoire (A&R). Find artists who inspire you and use each other to be the best you can be and to get your music out there.

Know Thy Business

If you don't know how you can make money as a songwriter then you have no business writing songs. I'm talking "mechanical rate," "three-quarter rate," "administration deal," "radio airplay," and "Mediabase." If you are unfamiliar with those words, immediately close this book, go to the bookstore, and buy a different book on the ins and out of the music publishing business. Be informed about the industry you are about to become a part of. Would you go to work anywhere without knowing what your salary will be or how you will get paid? Take the business side of songwriting and its risks seriously . . . it may make you reconsider your decision to be a songwriter.

Be a Music Consumer

Listen to all types of music and be inspired. Know what is currently popular in the market place and understand why. Study those songs and evaluate what makes them hit songs. Also remember to expose yourself to past great artists—the Beatles, Bob Dylan, the Stones. Let their genius move you and school you. You can learn from the writers who came before you.

Be Different

The key to today's songwriting is saying something universal in a different way. Don't just say I love you in the chorus. Give us a line that tells us that in an interesting way, "You can stand under my umbrella," as Rihanna puts it in "Umbrella." Don't just hem and haw about how someone missed a great opportunity. Get to the point: "If you like it then you should have put a ring on it," as Beyoncé sings in "Single Ladies." That's infinitely more interesting. Come into the room with a definitive standout concept hopefully based on something you have gone through so that it feels honest. Being unique combined with hooky melodies and smart lyrics is the path to big songs.

Give Back

Once you've succeeded in this business, help another artist/songwriter find his or her way. Mentorship is its own reward. Pay it forward.

Appendix B

RANDOM REFLECTIONS

There are so many more stories about my song-writing experiences that I haven't yet shared, I had to add just a few more here for your further amusement. My apologies to the many other phenomenal artists I've had the honor of working with—there just isn't enough room to recount all the good times, but I trust the memories are already in the music one way or another.

"Good Girls Go Bad"—Cobra Starship

It was ten o'clock in the morning the day of a results show during my first season of *Idol*. In my calendar it said "writing session with Cobra Starship." First off, I didn't like to cram sessions in on the day of *Idol* because I had to be on set by 1 P.M. On top of that, I had no idea who the band was, but my

assistant at the time, Katy (whom I mentioned before), did. She had sched-
uled me to work with them because she had a crush on the lead singer, Gabe.
She had a CD of theirs in her car with their music and quickly played it so
I'd have a point of reference.

What I didn't know was that Gabe was not used to cowriting and had
viewed my Web site in horror. He thought I was a cheesy pop writer and he
was a credible indie rock act. Needless to say, when I walked into the room
his "too cool for school" attitude permeated the room; I asked him if he had
any titles or ideas, and he went on to read some of the most vulgar combination of words (I can't put them on paper, or certain outlets won't take my
book). Of course I stared at him, stone-faced, and said, "What else you got?"
He said, " 'Good Girls Go Bad.' " Finally, a title that could play on radio.
Then he asked Kevin Rudolf (the producer/writer in the room) to pull up
some beats. Before I arrived, Gabe had instructed Kevin to play me all the
crappy ones first. He had no idea who he was dealing with; he was a cupcake
compared to the egos I had encountered over the years. As my Nanny Mary
used to say, I was going to fix his wagon.

On the first beat played, I started humming the chorus to "Good Girls
Go Bad." And all of a sudden Gabe was interested. He was coming closer
trying to hear what I was singing and looking pleasantly surprised. I told
him I had to leave to go shoot *Idol* and he asked if I could come back after-
ward. I said I would think about it and try to that evening. He was lucky he
was funny, and I sort of wanted to teach him that old don't-judge-a-book-
by-its-cover lesson. So I went back after *Idol* and we finished the song along
with Jacob Kasher. We are friends now and I love his music. He turned out
to be a great guy.

Adding Leighton Meester to the record took it to another level. I was a
fan of Leighton's from *Gossip Girl*, but I liked the real her infinitely more.

"Come Clean"—Hilary Duff

I had the title for this song in my back pocket, ready to pull it out when the time was right. The previous few years of writing had all been done to tracks. I stopped sitting down with musicians and just writing songs from the ground up. Instead, I was writing to "beds" of music (or tracks, as I have been referring to them), which in some ways were predestined for a certain theme or tone. I was particularly frustrated on my previous project because the tracks felt very uninspired and we had to write to them. Many had been a year or so old, which made their production value seem dated. I started to feel as if I was putting in hours at a corporation and just showing up for the paycheck. When I told everyone I thought we should write some new tracks or start a song on acoustic guitar, nobody listened and when you are stifled your work usually suffers.

"Come Clean" was a response to feeling that way. I decided to take a trip to California and meet some other songwriters. I was writing as if I were the artist; and the songs were all about what I was feeling. I didn't know that those songs would become valuable and sought after by other artists because they were so specific to what I was going through. "Come Clean" was one such song. It represented me breaking away from the heavy hand of others and their creative vision. It was a return to me and my own creativity, and it still struck a chord with Hilary. But that's what good songs do. They communicate unique perspectives in a universal way. I always cringe in the bridge when she sings "I'm coming"—she was like thirteen. That was just wrong.

"Confessions of a Broken Heart"—Lindsay Lohan

I had spent so many months with Lindsay and watched her suffer through her parents' fighting in the press and her own feelings of abandonment by her father. I felt very sorry for her. I had my own issues with my father (nothing like hers, though) and I could relate to her pain. I started the song for her, and it became a kind of soundtrack to her situation. It's one of the only songs I feel she really connected with on her second album and that she sang from her heart.

We recorded it in her rented summer house in the Hamptons, where I stayed for a few days to work with her. She rarely went to an actual studio to record vocals when I worked with her due to her hectic schedule. In fact, when we recorded her first album, I came up with the idea to set up a ministudio in her set trailer so she could work on breaks while she was filming *Herbie: Fully Loaded* at a racetrack in Fontana, California. That meant I would have to wait for hours, but that was the only way we could get the record delivered in time. If you solo the vocals, you can actually hear the race-car engines in the background.

"Screwed"—Paris Hilton

Paris wasn't the most seasoned singer. She'd even tell you that, but she worked diligently, standing in the vocal booth for hours on end, never asking for a break. I was really hard on her, and would tell her when her vocals needed to be better. I made her sing parts over and over and she never once acted like an heiress. She listened and tried her best. She was also very thoughtful. When she went for dinner she'd always ask if she could bring anything back for me. She was kind and generous. At the end of the record she thanked me and it was genuine. Got no beef with that girl. The only stress was when one of the producers, who had fallen in love with her, gave her a $500,000 necklace and it broke. She asked me if I could give it back to the jeweler as she wouldn't take it as a gift. I had to take back a broken necklace for her. Not fun. Luckily the jeweler hung out at the studio every day.

"Love Lives"—Steven Tyler

When my dear friend and hit songwriter/producer Marti Frederiksen called and asked what I was doing one afternoon in April 2010, I had coincidentally had a session blow out (sound familiar? Remember Pink's "Sober"?) He asked if he and Steven Tyler could come by and write. "Uh, what do you think?" I told him. Within thirty minutes, Steven Tyler was standing in my driveway and I was fixing my hair as if my prom date had just arrived. To say I was a fan was an understatement. I kept repeating, "I can't believe Steven Tyler is in my house." I only had a baby Taylor guitar and old Yamaha keyboard for him to play and he must have felt like he was driving a Yugo. But he never complained. Within minutes, he was singing "Dream On." I was pinching myself; how could this be happening? Steven said his father had been a classical pianist, which explained his use of range in that song.

I had nothing for him to eat, so I ordered pizza. I wanted to keep a piece of the crust sort of the way Marcia on *The Brandy Bunch* didn't want to wash her face after that groovy guy kissed her. The three of us wrote "Love Lives" that day, but I can't remember much of that. I mostly remember loving Steven, and Marti even more, for introducing me to this rock legend. He was funny, sweet, warm, and unbelievably humble. The best memory is when he met my father-in-law, who is from Maine and has a long beard, and he nicknamed him "Foliage Face." After our session, I mentioned Steven to one of the producers at *Idol* as a possible replacement for Simon Cowell and connected them.

"Beep"—Pussycat Dolls

One of the best producer/writer/artists I have ever worked with is will.i.am. He is walking, breathing genius. When I arrived at the studio he had the chorus to "Beep" already laid down. It was a reaction to his label and radio programmers wanting to change the title of his song "Don't Phunk with My Heart" on the Black Eyed Peas *Monkey Business* album due to the controversial usage of the word "phunk" in the title (i.e., "Don't f**k with my heart"). He figured why not create a song where all words of suspect were already bleeped out; that way no one could ever censor his thoughts. He was so generous and encouraging in the room. I met a lot of extraordinary people writing songs for the Pussycat Dolls. I adored Nicole Scherzinger from the moment I met her. I still have the bra she gave me that day in the studio when the cameras were rolling and you could see straight through my shirt. She literally took it off her body and gave it to me. It's still the best damn bra I got. Take that for memorabilia.

"Lost"

As I've mentioned, some songs just come to you. You'll be sitting there speaking to a friend and all of a sudden a chorus will hit you. That's what happened with "Lost." I was out on my deck having a glass of red wine with my dear friend and cowriter Mitch Allan, enjoying the moment. We were speaking about something completely unrelated to music and I said "Oh my God, can you grab your guitar?" I heard the entire chorus in my head and sang it to him so he could find the right chords. I was so suspect of this song that just sort of popped into my head that I didn't want to finish it. I thought it must have flaws if it came to me under such strange circumstances. Maybe I was scared of its power over me. It's a little odd when you hear a voice in your head that's a chorus to a song while you're in the middle of doing something totally unrelated. Mitch was on me to complete it. I was extremely reluctant but did. I got the call driving that it would be Faith Hill's single. It was our first country cut.

"I Never Told You"—Colbie Caillat

One of the most beautiful places I have ever written in is Kauai, Hawaii. Colbie Caillat invited me to work with her there for a few days in January 2009. She rented a beautiful beach house where we (there were other great writers there, too, including Jason Reeves and Mikal Blue) slept, ate, swam, and of course wrote music. There was magic all around. Every day began with a rainbow and every night ended with an acoustic set in the common living room. It was all-around paradise.

One morning I heard Colbie upstairs singing in her room and it was so utterly breathtaking. Her voice is like warm honey. I was not familiar with the song, and asked her what it was. She said it was something she had started writing. She was singing the nucleus of what would become "I Never Told You." She was a bit shy about her creation, but Jason Reeves and I convinced her to sing it for us again. She asked us to finish the song with her. Then we all went for a swim. Writing had never felt more like paradise.

Until the next morning, when I woke up and the mosquitoes had feasted on my face. I had about ten huge bites. I am crazy about washing my face and taking care of my skin, as I am prone to breaking out. It looked as if I had ten huge teenage pimples. I wanted to die. Not to mention I was flying to NYC in three days to be on *Late Night with David Letterman* to promote Season 8 of *Idol*. Colbie tried to calm me down, saying it wasn't that bad, but I could see fear in everyone's eyes. I walked around with a huge can of insect repellent, spraying myself every hour on the hour for the next two days. Luckily when I got out of the humidity and hit New York City, the bumps went down. Now sometimes when I hear the song on the radio, I can't help but laugh.

"This"—Darius Rucker

I was an avid Hootie fan, and if someone had told me ten years ago that I would be writing a country song with Darius Rucker over iChat I would never have believed them. Darius, Frank Rogers, and I actually wrote "This" for Darius's *Charleston, SC 1966* album that way. Darius seemed so grateful for all he had and this song celebrates the good and bad in everyone's lives, for without both, some of us might not be in the better place we are today. He definitely seemed to be in a great place and thankfully I could relate to "This'" sentiment finding myself content after years of unrest.

Appendix C

AWARDS

NAMM Music for Life Award—2011

SOCAN Pop/Rock Music Award—2010 ("Not Meant to Be," Theory of a Deadman)

BMI Pop Music Awards—2010 ("I Do Not Hook Up," Kelly Clarkson)

BMI Pop Music Awards—2010 ("Sober," Pink)

BMI Pop Music Awards—2010 ("Not Meant to Be," Theory of a Deadman)

NMPA Songwriter Icon Award—2009

BMI Latin Pop Music Awards—2009 ("Somebody's Me," Enrique Iglesias)

BMI Latin Pop Music Awards—2008 ("Bella Traición," Belinda)

BMI Pop Music Awards—2008 ("Ain't No Other Man," Christina Aguilera)

Columbus Citizens Foundation Award—2007—Outstanding Contribution to the Vocal Arts

SOCAN Pop Award—2007 ("Walk Away," Kelly Clarkson)

All of the information in this section comes from various published sources, including *Billboard* magazine, AOL Radio Charts (via www.billboard.com), iTunes Charts, the Official Charts Company (UK), Nielsen SoundScan, Mediabase, RIAA, ARIA, CRIA, RIANZ, the Swiss Singles Charts, the Italian Singles Charts, the Ireland Singles Charts, the German Singles Charts, and the Austrian Singles Charts and reflects rankings at the time of this book's production.

TAXI Award—2007 Humanitarian of the Year

BMI Pop Music Awards—2007 Songwriter of the Year

BMI Pop Music Awards—2006 ("I'm Feeling You," Santana)

BMI Pop Music Awards—2006 ("Walk Away," Kelly Clarkson)

BMI Pop Music Awards—2006 ("The Real Thing," Bo Bice)

BMI Pop Music Awards—2005 ("Pieces of Me," Ashlee Simpson)

BMI Pop Music Awards—2005 ("Rich Girl," Gwen Stefani)

BMI Pop Music Awards—2002 ("Escape," Enrique Iglesias)

BMI Top Ten Latin Award—2002 ("Escapar," Enrique Iglesias)

BMI Film & TV Music Awards—2003 (*For the People* theme song)

Appendix D

U.S. SINGLES

"This" (Darius Rucker)
#12 Billboard Country Songs
#81 Billboard Hot 100
#64 Billboard Radio Songs

"Undo It" (Carrie Underwood)
#1 Billboard Hot Country
#1 Country Mediabase Charts
#23 Billboard Hot 100

"I Never Told You" (Colbie Caillat)
#3 Billboard Adult Top 40
#3 AOL Radio
#11 Billboard Hot Adult Contemporary
#48 Billboard Hot 100

"Mama's Song" (Carrie Underwood)
#2 Billboard Hot Country
#22 iTunes Top Songs
#56 Billboard Hot 100

"He Could Be the One" (Hannah Montana)
#4 iTunes Top Songs
#10 Billboard Hot 100

"Good Girls Go Bad" (Cobra Starship)
#4 iTunes Top Songs
#7 Billboard Hot 100
#5 Billboard Pop Songs
#25 Hot AC

"Hot Mess" (Cobra Starship)
#14 iTunes Top Songs
#25 Billboard Digital Songs
#64 Billboard Hot 100

"No Boundaries" (Kris Allen)
#11 Billboard Hot 100
#19 Hot AC

"I Do Not Hook Up" (Kelly Clarkson)
#8 Billboard Top 40
#13 Billboard Hot AC
#12 Billboard Pop 100
#20 Billboard Hot Digital
#20 Billboard Hot 100

"Sober" (Pink)
#1 Hot AC
#2 Adult Top 40
#4 Top 40
#15 Billboard Hot 100

"Not Meant to Be" (Theory of a Deadman)
#4 Hot AC
#6 Adult Top 40
#23 Top 40
#55 Billboard Hot 100

"Wanted" (Jessie James)
#22 Top 40
#35 Hot AC
#40 Billboard Hot 100

"Play My Music" (Jonas Brothers)
#7 Hot Digital Songs
#20 Billboard Hot 100

"We Rock" (Camp Rock Cast)
#33 Billboard Hot 100

"Taking Chances" (Céline Dion)
#6 Hot AC
#35 Billboard Pop 100
#54 Billboard Hot 100

"Lost" (Faith Hill)
#11 Billboard Hot AC
#32 Billboard Hot Country Songs
#51 Billboard Pop 100
#61 Hot 100

"Baby Love" (Nicole Scherzinger)
#50 Billboard Pop 100
#4 Billboard Dance/Club Play Songs

"Rich Girl" (Gwen Stefani)
#3 Billboard Pop 100
#4 Top 40
#7 Billboard Hot 100

"Ain't No Other Man" (Christina Aguilera)
#1 Top 40
#1 Billboard Dance
#4 Billboard Pop 100
#6 Billboard Hot 100

"Walk Away" (Kelly Clarkson)
#6 Billboard Pop 100
#12 Billboard Hot 100
#19 Billboard AC

"Beep" (Pussycat Dolls)
#12 Top 40
#13 Billboard Hot 100

"I'm Feeling You" (Santana featuring Michelle Branch)
#5 Billboard AC
#53 Billboard Pop 100
#55 Billboard Hot 100

"With Love" (Hilary Duff)
#3 Hot Digital Airplay
#17 Billboard Pop 100
#24 Billboard Hot 100

"Come Clean" (Hilary Duff)
#9 Top 40
#35 Billboard Hot 100

"L.O.V.E." (Ashlee Simpson)
#20 Billboard Pop 100
#22 Billboard Hot 100

"Boyfriend" (Ashlee Simpson)
#13 Billboard Pop 100
#19 Billboard Hot 100

"Pieces of Me" (Ashlee Simpson)
#5 Billboard Hot 100
#30 Billboard AC

"Shadow" (Ashlee Simpson)
#57 Billboard Hot 100

"La La" (Ashlee Simpson)
#6 Billboard Dance
#86 Billboard Hot 100

"Escape" / "Escapar" (Enrique Iglesias)
#1 Billboard Dance
#2 Hot Latin
#12 Billboard Hot 100
#25 Billboard AC

"Be Good to Me" (Ashley Tisdale)
#80 Billboard Hot 100

"Bella Traición" (Belinda)
#11 Billboard Latin Tropical Airplay
#13 Billboard Latin Pop Airplay
#14 Billboard Hot Latin Songs

"The Real Thing" (Bo Bice)
#17 Billboard AC
#33 Billboard Pop 100
#56 Billboard Hot 100

"Confessions of a Broken Heart" (Lindsay Lohan)
#12 Billboard Pop 100
#57 Billboard Hot 100

"The Way" (Clay Aiken)
#4 U.S. Charts

Appendix E

INTERNATIONAL SINGLES

"Mama's Song" (Carrie Underwood)
#68 Canadian Hot 100

"Ghost" (Fefe Dobson)
#14 Canadian Hot 100

"Undo It" (Carrie Underwood)
#28 Canadian Country Singles Chart
#43 Canadian Hot 100

"Good Girls Go Bad" (Cobra Starship)
#2 NZ Singles Chart
#5 Australian Singles Chart
#7 Canadian Hot 100
#17 UK Singles Chart

"Hot Mess" (Cobra Starship)
#40 NZ Singles Chart
#58 Canadian Hot 100

"He Could Be the One" (Hannah Montana)
#64 Australian Singles Chart
#97 Canadian Hot 100

"I Do Not Hook Up" (Kelly Clarkson)
#9 Australian Singles Chart
#13 Canadian Hot 100
#31 NZ Singles Chart
#36 UK Singles Chart

"Sober" (Pink)
#4 Australian Singles Chart
#8 Canadian Singles Chart
#9 UK Singles Chart
Top ten in 11 Countries

"Play My Music" (Jonas Brothers)
#57 UK Singles Chart

"Come Clean" (Hilary Duff)
#7 Canadian Singles Chart
#17 Australian Singles Chart
#17 NZ Singles Chart
#18 UK Singles Chart

"Pieces of Me" (Ashlee Simpson)
#4 UK Singles Chart
#7 Australian Singles Chart
#32 NZ Singles Chart

"La La" (Ashlee Simpson)
#10 Australian Singles Chart
#11 UK Singles Chart
#11 NZ Singles Chart

"Boyfriend" (Ashlee Simpson)
#8 Australian Singles Chart
#12 UK Singles Chart
#21 NZ Singles Chart

"Taking Chances" (Céline Dion)
Top ten in 7 Countries
#1 Canadian Hot 100
#12 European Singles Chart
#26 World Singles
#40 UK Singles Chart

"Sunshine" (Ricki-Lee Coulter)
#1 Australian Singles Chart

"Ain't No Other Man" (Christina Aguilera)
Top ten in 12 countries
#2 UK Singles Chart
#4 Canadian Hot 100

"Rich Girl" (Gwen Stefani)
Top ten in 12 countries
#2 European Hot 100
#4 Canadian Hot 100

"Beep" (Pussycat Dolls)
Top ten in 14 countries
#2 UK Singles Chart

"I Don't Need a Man" (Pussycat Dolls)
#7 UK Singles Chart
Top ten in 9 countries

"Escape" (Enrique Iglesias)
#3 UK Singles Chart
#5 Australian Singles Chart
#24 NZ Singles Chart

"Maybe" (Enrique Iglesias)
#12 UK Singles Chart
#29 NZ Singles Chart

"Don't Turn Off the Lights" (Enrique Iglesias)
#4 Australia Singles Chart
#6 NZ Singles Chart

"I Belong to You" (Anastacia and Eros Ramazzotti)
#1 Italian and Swiss Singles Charts
#3 European Hot 100 Singles

"Spinning Around" (Kylie Minogue)
#1 UK and Australia hit
Top ten in 10 countries

"Walk Away" (Kelly Clarkson)
Top ten in 13 countries
#21 UK Singles Chart

"Welcome to My Truth" (Anastacia)
Top ten in 4 countries

"One Heart" (Céline Dion)
#13 Canada Singles Chart
#27 UK Singles Chart

"Predictable" (Delta Goodrem)
#1 Australia Singles Chart

"Not Me, Not I" (Delta Goodrem)
#1 Australia Singles Chart

"Confessions of a Broken Heart" (Lindsay Lohan)
#7 Australia Singles Chart

"Over" (Lindsay Lohan)
#27 UK Singles Chart

"I've Got You" (Martine McCutcheon)
#6 UK hit

"Cry Baby Cry" (Santana)
#15 Canadian Hot 100
#71 UK Singles Chart

"Someone's Watching Over Me" (Hilary Duff)
#22 Australian Singles Chart

"Alguien Real" (Thalia)
Top twenty in 5 countries

"Kinda Love" (Darius)
#8 UK Singles Chart

"Shut Up" (Kelly Osbourne)
#11 UK Singles Charts
Top twenty in Ireland and Norway

"No Boundaries" (Kris Allen)
#13 Canadian Hot 100
#92 UK Singles Chart

"Not Meant to Be" (Theory of a Deadman)
#53 Canadian Hot 100

"We Rock" (Camp Rock)
#41 Canadian Hot 100

"Lost" (Faith Hill)
#40 Canadian Hot 100

"Baby Love" (Nicole Scherzinger)
#14 UK Singles Chart
#5 Germany Singles Chart
#15 Ireland Singles Chart
Top ten in 6 countries

"With Love" (Hilary Duff)
#6 Canadian Hot 100
#19 UK Singles Chart
#22 Australian Singles Chart
Top ten in 4 countries

"Be Good to Me" (Ashley Tisdale)
#67 Austria Singles Chart
#57 Germany Singles Chart

"L.O.V.E." (Ashlee Simpson)
#5 Australian Singles Chart
#16 New Zealand Singles Chart

"Shadow" (Ashlee Simpson)
#31 Australian Singles Chart
#42 German Singles Chart

Appendix F

TOP-TEN ALBUMS

Charleston, SC 1966 (Darius Rucker)
1 single
#1 Billboard Top Country Albums
#2 Billboard 200
#1 iTunes Album Chart

The Band Perry (The Band Perry)
1 song
#4 Billboard 200
#2 Billboard Top Country Albums
#8 iTunes Album Chart

Camp Rock 2: The Final Jam (Soundtrack)
1 song
#3 Billboard 200
#1 U.S. Billboard Top Soundtracks

Hang Cool Teddy Bear (Meat Loaf)

1 song

#3 Billboard 200

#2 Billboard Rock Albums

#1 Billboard Canadian Albums

Jonas L.A. (Soundtrack)

1 song

#2 Billboard 200

Pulse (Toni Braxton)

1 song

#1 Billboard R&B/Hip-Hop Albums

#9 Billboard 200

My Best Days (Danny Gokey)

1 song

#4 Billboard 200

#3 Billboard Top Country Album

2010 Grammy Nominees Album

1 song

#5 Billboard 200

For Your Entertainment (Adam Lambert)

1 song

#3 Billboard 200

Play On (Carrie Underwood)

2 singles

#1 Billboard 200

#1 Top Country Album

Glee: Season One: The Music Volume 1 (Glee)
1 song
#4 Billboard 200

NOW 32
1 song
#5 Billboard 200

The Time of Our Lives (Miley Cyrus)
1 song
#2 Billboard 200

Breakthrough (Colbie Caillat)
4 songs: 1 single
#1 Billboard 200

Hot Mess (Cobra Starship)
2 singles
#4 Billboard 200

Hannah Montana 3 Soundtrack
4 songs: 2 singles
#2 Billboard 200

Hannah Montana: The Movie Soundtrack
1 song
#1 Billboard 200
#1 Top Country Album

NOW 30
1 song
#1 Billboard 200

All I Ever Wanted (Kelly Clarkson)
1 single
#1 Billboard 200

Unstoppable (Rascal Flatts)
1 song
#1 Billboard 200
#1 Top Country Album

It Keeps Getting Better: A Decade of Hits (Christina Aguilera)
1 song
#9 Billboard 200

Funhouse (Pink)
1 single
#2 Billboard 200

David Archuleta (David Archuleta)
1 song
#2 Billboard 200

My Love: Essential Collection (Céline Dion)
1 song
#8 Billboard 200

Don't Forget (Demi Lovato)
2 songs
#1 Top Internet Sales
#2 Billboard 200
#2 Top Digital

Doll Domination (Pussycat Dolls)
2 songs
#4 Billboard 200
#3 Top Digital

Camp Rock (Various Artists)
2 singles
#2 Top Digital
#3 Billboard 200

Taking Chances (Céline Dion)
3 songs: 1 single
#1 European Album Charts
#3 Billboard 200
Top ten in 22 Countries

Blackout (Britney Spears)
1 song
#2 Billboard 200

Unbreakable (Backstreet Boys)
1 song
#7 Billboard 200

Spirit (Leona Lewis)
1 song (Japanese Bonus Track)
#6 European Hot 100 Albums

Kidz Bop 12
1 song
#7 Billboard 200

Hannah Montana 2 (Hannah Montana)
1 song
#1 Billboard 200

My December (Kelly Clarkson)
1 single
#1 Top Digital
#2 Billboard 200
#2 Top Internet
#5 European Top 100

El Cartel: The Big Boss (Daddy Yankee)
1 song
#1 Top Latin
#9 Billboard 200

Best Damn Thing (Avril Lavigne)
1 song
#1 Billboard 200
#1 European Top 100
#1 Top Digital Album
Top ten in 31 Countries

Taylor Hicks (Taylor Hicks)
2 songs: 1 single
#2 Billboard 200
#2 Top Internet

Headstrong (Ashley Tisdale)
1 single
#5 Billboard 200
#5 Top Internet

Insomniac (Enrique Iglesias)
3 songs: 1 single
#3 UK Top 200
Top ten in 4 countries

Love. Angel. Music. Baby. (Gwen Stefani)
1 single
#2 Billboard 200
Top ten in 9 countries

Back to Basics (Christina Aguilera)
12 songs: 1 single
#1 Billboard 200
#2 Top R&B Hip-Hop

Breakaway (Kelly Clarkson)
6 songs: 1 single
#3 Billboard 200

One Heart (Céline Dion)
2 songs: 1 single
#2 Billboard 200
Top ten in 29 Countries
#1 in 9 Countries

A New Day Has Come (Céline Dion)
2 songs
#1 Billboard 200

Goodbye Alice in Wonderland (Jewel)
1 single
#8 Billboard 200

All That I Am (Santana)
2 songs: 1 single
#2 Billboard 200

What's Left of Me (Nick Lachey)
1 song
#2 Billboard 200

In the Zone (Britney Spears)
1 song
#1 Debut Billboard 200

Ultimate Kylie (Kylie Minogue)
1 single
Top ten in 5 countries

PCD (Pussycat Dolls)
3 songs: 2 singles
#5 Billboard 200

Life (Ricky Martin)
1 song
#6 Billboard 200
#6 Top Internet

Autobiography (Ashlee Simpson)
8 songs: 3 singles
#1 Billboard 200

I Am Me (Ashlee Simpson)
11 songs: 2 singles
#1 Billboard 200

Most Wanted (Hilary Duff)

1 song

#1 Billboard 200

Metamorphosis (Hilary Duff)

2 songs: 1 single

#1 Billboard 200

Hilary Duff (Hilary Duff)

5 songs: 2 singles

#2 Billboard 200

Dignity (Hilary Duff)

12 songs: 3 singles

#3 Billboard 200

Escape (Enrique Iglesias)

7 songs: 3 singles

#2 Billboard 200

Anastacia (Anastacia)

6 songs: 1 single

#1 European record

Top five in 16 countries

Pieces of a Dream (Anastacia)

2 songs: 1 single

#6 UK Album Chart

Irresistible (Jessica Simpson)

1 single

#6 Billboard 200

Measure of a Man (Clay Aiken)
1 single
#1 Billboard 200

Mended (Marc Anthony)
10 songs: 2 singles
#3 Billboard 200

Thalia (Thalia)
2 singles
#2 Top Latin

NOW 23
1 song
#1 Billboard 200

Paris (Paris Hilton)
4 songs
#6 Billboard 200

Innocent Eyes (Delta Goodrem)
2 songs: 2 singles
#1 Australia

Katharine McPhee (Katharine McPhee)
6 songs: 1 single
#2 Billboard 200

Speak (Lindsay Lohan)
6 songs: 2 singles
#4 Billboard 200

Take It All Away (Ryan Cabrera)
1 single
#6 Billboard 200
#1 in 9 countries

You, Me & Us (Martine McCutcheon)
1 single
#2 UK Album Charts

The Real Thing (Bo Bice)
3 songs: 2 singles
#4 Billboard 200

A Cinderella Story: Original Soundtrack (Hilary Duff)
1 song
#9 Billboard 200

Appendix G

SOUNDTRACKS AND SONGS ON FILM

Camp Rock 2: The Final Jam (Disney 2010)—"Brand New Day" (Demi Lovato)

Youth in Revolt (Dimension Films 2010)—"L.O.V.E." (Ashlee Simpson)

Hannah Montana: The Movie (Disney 2009)—"Dream Dream Dream" (Miley Cyrus)

Confessions of a Shopaholic (Touchstone 2009)—"Rich Girl" (Gwen Stefani)

Céline Dion Through the Eyes of the World (Sony 2009)—"Taking Chances" (Céline Dion)

Alvin and the Chipmunks 2 (20th Century Fox 2009)—"Ain't No Other Man" (Christina Aguilera)

Paris Not France (MTV 2009)—"Jealousy" (Paris Hilton)

Camp Rock (Disney 2008)—"We Rock" (Cast of *Camp Rock*)

Beverly Hills Chihuahua (Disney 2008)—"Rich Girl" (Gwen Stefani)

Get Smart (Warner Bros. 2008)—"Ain't No Other Man" (Christina Aguilera)

Welcome Home Roscoe Jenkins (Universal 2008)—"Ain't No Other Man" (Christina Aguilera)

Bring It On: In It to Win It (Universal 2007)—"Never Stop" (Hilary Duff) and "Be Good To Me" (Ashley Tisdale)

Bratz (Lions Gate 2007)—"La La" (Ashlee Simpson)

Bring It On: All or Nothing (Universal 2006)—"Rich Girl" (Gwen Stefani)

Last Holiday (Paramount 2006)—"Rich Girl" (Gwen Stefani)

Herbie: Fully Loaded (Disney 2005)—"First" (Lindsay Lohan)

Ice Princess (Disney 2005)—"Reach" (Caleigh Peters)

Raise Your Voice (New Line Cinema 2004)—"Someone's Watching Over Me" (Hilary Duff) and "Fly" (Hilary Duff)

A Cinderella Story (Warner Bros. 2004)—"Now You Know" (Hilary Duff)

Scooby-Doo 2: Monsters Unleashed (Warner Bros. 2004)—"The Way" (Clay Aiken)

Confessions of a Teenage Drama Queen (Disney 2004)—"Ready" (Cherie) and "1-2-3" (Nikki Cleary)

Appendix H

THEME SONGS AND SONGS ON TELEVISION

Theme song for *Laguna Beach* and *Newport Harbor*—"Come Clean" (Hilary Duff)

Theme song for *The Ashlee Simpson Show*—"Autobiography" (Ashlee Simpson)

The Hills—"Black Hole" (Lindsay Lohan), "Fast Lane" (Suzie McNeil), "I Do Not Hook Up" (Kelly Clarkson), and "I Never Told You" (Colbie Caillat)

The City—"Cold Front" (Amie Miriello), "Good Girls Go Bad" (Cobra Starship), and "Hot Mess" (Cobra Starship)

CSI: Miami—"Good Girls Go Bad" (Cobra Starship)

Cold Case—"Hear Me" (Kelly Clarkson)

One Tree Hill—"All in My Head" (Nick Lachey)

Gossip Girl—"Good Girls Go Bad" (Cobra Starship)

90210—"Wanted" (Jessie James)

Will & Grace—"I Will Remember You" (Ryan Cabrera)

Drop Dead Diva—"I Do Not Hook Up" (Kelly Clarkson)

Glee—"Taking Chances" (Céline Dion)

Greek—"Good Girls Go Bad" (Cobra Starship)

Ugly Betty—"Good Girls Go Bad" (Cobra Starship)

Celebrity Circus—"Come Clean" (Hilary Duff)

High School Musical: Get in the Picture—"All in My Head" (Nick Lachey)

7th Heaven—"Good Day" (Jewel)

The Real Housewives of Orange County—"Hot Mess" (Cobra Starship)

Beauty and the Geek—"Believe" (Suzie McNeil)

Living Lohan—"All the Way Around" (Ali Lohan) and "Close That Door"
    (Ali Lohan)

MTV's *10 on Top*—"Ghost" (Fefe Dobson)

Extreme Makeover Home Edition—"What If" (Ashley Tisdale)

VH1's *I Love the New Millennium*—"The Way" (Clay Aiken) and "Come
    Clean" (Hilary Duff)

E! Entertainment Special: *Christina Aguilera*—"Ain't No Other Man"
    (Christina Aguilera) and "Oh Mother" (Christina Aguilera)

American Idol—"Sometimes You Leave" (Carrie Underwood), "I Will Re-
    member You" (Ryan Cabrera), "No Boundaries" (Kris Allen), "Not Ur
    Girl" (Katharine McPhee), "Terrified" (Katharine McPhee), "Sober"
    (Pink), "Where Is Your Heart" (Kelly Clarkson), "Had It All" (Katha-
    rine McPhee), "Walk Away" (Kelly Clarkson), "Undo It" (Carrie Under-
    wood), "I'm Ready" (Cherie), and "I've Got You" (Martine McCutcheon)

So You Think You Can Dance—"Cold Front" (Amie Miriello), "I Do Not
    Hook Up" (Kelly Clarkson), "Good Girls Go Bad" (Cobra Starship),
    and "I Will Remember You" (Ryan Cabrera)

America's Got Talent—"Dream Dream Dream" (Miley Cyrus)

America's Best Dance Crew—"Hot Mess" (Cobra Starship)

Dancing with the Stars—"Taking Chances" (Céline Dion)

America's Next Top Model—"Good Girls Go Bad" (Cobra Starship)

The Biggest Loser—"Best of Me" (Daniel Powter)

The Ellen DeGeneres Show—"Rich Girl" (Gwen Stefani), "Pieces of Me" (Ashlee Simpson), "With Love" (Hilary Duff), "Walk Away" (Kelly Clarkson), "L.O.V.E." (Ashlee Simpson), "I Do Not Hook Up" (Kelly Clarkson), "No Boundaries" (Kris Allen), "Good Girls Go Bad" (Cobra Starship), "Wanted" (Jessie James), and "Terrified" (Katharine McPhee)

The Oprah Winfrey Show—"Strut" (Adam Lambert)

The Tonight Show with Conan O'Brien—"Good Girls Go Bad" (Cobra Starship) and "Had It All" (Katharine McPhee)

The Tonight Show with Jay Leno—"I Do Not Hook Up" (Kelly Clarkson) and "Give a Little Love" (Tom Jones), "Terrified" (Katharine McPhee), "I Never Told You" (Colbie Caillat), and "Ain't No Other Man" (Christina Aguilera)

Late Night with Jimmy Fallon—"Never" (Tom Jones)

Lopez Tonight—"Terrified" (Kara and Jason Reeves live performance) and "Stranger" (Hilary Duff)

Jimmy Kimmel Live—"Hot Mess" (Cobra Starship), "Good Girls Go Bad" (Cobra Starship), "Undo It" (Carrie Underwood), and "I Never Told You" (Colbie Caillat)

The Bonnie Hunt Show—"Do It For You" (Ballas Hough Band) and "Terrified" (Katharine McPhee)

The Late Show with David Letterman—"Terrified" (Katharine McPhee)

Appendix I

CAMPAIGNS AND COMMERCIALS

"Good Girls Go Bad" (Cobra Starship)—Trailer and Promo for *You Again* (Touchstone 2010)

"Give a Little Love" (Tom Jones)—Trailer and Promo for *Little Fockers* (Universal 2010)

"Rich Girl" (Gwen Stefani)—Pepsi Campaign

"Believe" (Suzie McNeil)—Bell Canada Olympic Games Campaign

"Taking Chances" (Céline Dion) and "Believe" (Suzie McNeil)—*Biggest Loser* Promo Campaign

"My Bra" (Mya)—Lifetime Television's Breast Cancer Awareness Campaign

"With Love" (Hilary Duff)—Hilary Duff/Elizabeth Arden Perfume Commercial

"A Little Bit" (Jessica Simpson)—Bally's Total Fitness Campaign

"Good Day" (Jewel)—Extreme Makeover Campaign

"Supergirl" (Miley Cyrus)—Candies Campaign

"One Heart" (Céline Dion)—Chrysler Campaign

"Don't Turn Off the Lights" (Enrique Iglesias)—Doritos Campaign

"I'm Ready" (Cherie)—Dell Campaign

"La La" (Ashlee Simpson)—Thermasilk Campaign

"Give a Little Love" (Tom Jones)—Telecom Italia Commercial

"I Don't Need a Man" (Pussycat Dolls)—C&A Clothing Commercial

"With Love" (Hilary Duff)—Cartier Love Charity Project

"Believe" (Suzie McNeil)—Sears Campaign

"Believe" (Suzie McNeil)—United Way Internet Commercial

"Come Clean" (Hilary Duff) and "With Love" (Hilary Duff)—Times Square Style Series (online)

Permissions

LYRICS

WB Music Corp. All rights reserved. Used by permission. Reprinted by permission of Hal Leonard Corporation.

"Hook Up" A/K/A "I Don't Hook Up"
Words and music by Katy Perry, Greg Wells, and Kara DioGuardi. © 2009 When I'm Rich You'll Be My Bitch, Art in the Fodder Music, Rocket Carousel Music, and K'tuff Publishing. All rights on behalf of When I'm Rich You'll Be My Bitch. Administered by WB Music Corp. All rights reserved. Used by permission.

Page 105   Chapter Eight   "Walk Away"
"Walk Away"
Words and music by Kelly Clarkson, Chantal Kreviazuk, Raine Maida, and Kara DioGuardi. © 2004 Smelly Songs, Sony/ATV Music Publishing Canada, Neverwouldathot Music and Bug Music Inc. All rights for Smelly Songs controlled and administered by EMI April Music Inc. All rights for Sony/ATV Music Publishing Canada and Neverwouldathot Music administered by Sony/ATV Music Publishing LLC, 8 Music Square West, Nashville, TN 37203. All rights reserved. International copyright secured. Used by permission. Reprinted by permission of Hal Leonard Corporation.

"Walk Away"
Copyright 2004 Sony/ATV Music Publishing Canada, Neverwouldathot Music LLC, Under Zenith Music L.L.C., K'Stuff Publishing, BMG Songs Inc. All rights on behalf of Sony/ATV Music Publishing Canada, Neverwouldathot Music LLC, and Under Zenith Music L.L.C. administered by Sony/ATV Music Publishing LLC, 8 Music Square West, Nashville, TN 37203. All rights reserved. Used by permission.

PHOTOGRAPHS

Photograph by Brian Ach, courtesy of Getty Images insert p. 9, bottom center

Photograph by Andre Canaparo insert p. 5, bottom

Photograph by Lester Cohen, courtesy of Getty Images insert p. 6, top left

From the personal archives of Kara DioGuardi: insert p. 1, top left; insert p. 1, top right; insert p. 1, center left; insert p. 1, bottom right; insert p. 2, top left; insert p. 2, top right; insert p. 2, center left; insert p. 2, center right; insert p. 3, top left; insert p. 3, center right; insert p. 13, bottom left; insert p. 13, bottom right; insert p. 15, top; insert p. 16, top

Photograph by Ned Douglas, courtesy of Dave Stewart insert p. 3, bottom left

Photograph by Stephen J. Finfer insert p. 4, top right; insert p. 4, center left; insert p. 5, top left; insert p. 5, center left; insert p. 6, center left; insert p. 7, center left; insert p. 7, bottom right; insert p. 8, top right; insert p. 8, center right; insert p. 9, top left; insert p. 10, top left; insert p. 10, bottom; insert p. 11, top; insert p. 11, bottom; insert p. 12, bottom; insert p. 13, top; insert p. 14, top right; insert p. 14, bottom left; insert p. 14, bottom right; insert p. 15, center; insert p. 15, bottom; insert p. 16, bottom

Photograph by Dean Hendler © by Disney Channel insert p. 7, top right

Photograph by Robert Lurie, courtesy of Phoenix House insert p. 11, center

Photograph by Lester Millman insert p. 2, bottom left

Photograph courtesy of StudioBooth, www.thestudiobooth.com insert p. 4, bottom right; insert p. 9, top right

Photograph by Justine Ungaro insert p. 12, top

Photograph by Greg Wells insert p. 6, bottom right

Photograph by Kevin Winter/American Idol 2009, courtesy of Getty Images insert p. 8, bottom left

About the Author

While you may know her from her role as a judge on *American Idol* Seasons 8 and 9, Kara is one of the industry's most sought-after songwriters and producers. Her songs have appeared on more than 159 million albums. Kara is a Grammy-nominated hitmaker, 2011 NAMM Music for Life Award winner, 2009 NMPA Songwriter Icon Award winner, 2007 BMI Pop Songwriter of the Year, and has received 15 BMI Awards for cowriting the most-performed songs on the radio. Kara also works at Warner Bros. Records, where she serves as Executive VP of Talent Development, Office of the Chairman, and has signed along with Beluga Heights such hit artists as Jason Derulo and Iyaz. Further, Kara co-owns Arthouse Entertainment, a music-publishing venture, with Bug Music, which has published such hits as: B.O.B's "Nothin' on You," Bruno Mars' "Just the Way You Are" and "Grenade," Cee-Lo Green's "Forget You," and Flo Rida's "Club Can't Handle Me." Kara is also currently appearing as a judge on *Platinum Hit*, Bravo's new reality show in search of America's best songwriters.

Kara's most recent songwriting releases cover a variety of music genres and include Darius Rucker's "This," Colbie Caillat's "I Never Told You," Carrie Underwood's "Undo It" and "Mama's Song," Pink's "Sober," Kelly Clarkson's "I Do Not Hook Up," Cobra Starship featuring Leighton Meester's "Good Girls Go Bad," and Theory of a Deadman's "Not Meant to Be," among others.

More than 305 of her songs have been released on major labels and nearly 150 of those have appeared on platinum-selling albums. Throughout her career, she has had more than 40 worldwide charting singles, and her songs have helped propel more than 65 albums into the Top Ten of the Billboard 200. Kara's songs are continuously featured in major motion pictures, television shows, film soundtracks, and radio spots, as well as national and international commercial campaigns.

Kara's songs have been recorded by Grammy Award–winning artists such as Pink, Carrie Underwood, Christina Aguilera, Gwen Stefani, Kelly Clarkson, Céline Dion, Rascal Flatts, Colbie Caillat, Santana, Faith Hill, Darius Rucker, Toni Braxton, Meat Loaf, and Marc Anthony. Many other major recording artists have also released Kara's songs, including Britney Spears, Avril Lavigne, Enrique Iglesias, Jonas Brothers, Adam Lambert, Leona Lewis, Hannah Montana, Miley Cyrus, Natasha Bedingfield, Jewel, Demi Lovato, Kris Allen, Theory of a Deadman, Cobra Starship, Pussycat Dolls, Ricky Martin, Puddle of Mudd, Ashley Tisdale, Katharine McPhee, David Archuleta, Camp Rock, Allison Iraheta, Bo Bice, Clay Aiken, Crystal Bowersox, Jesse McCartney, Backstreet Boys, Ashlee Simpson, Hilary Duff, Tom Jones, Jessica Simpson, Nick Lachey, Jo Dee Messina, Paula Abdul, and Daddy Yankee. DioGuardi has achieved equal success internationally with hit singles for artists such as Anastacia, Kylie Minogue, Diego, Belinda, RBD, Eros Ramazzotti, Delta Goodrem, Darius, Thalia, and Martine McCutcheon.

Kara's coproduction credits include Kelly Clarkson, Céline Dion, Britney Spears, Santana, Hannah Montana, Camp Rock, Jonas Brothers, Adam Lambert, Hilary Duff, Kylie Minogue, the Pussycat Dolls, the Backstreet Boys, Katharine McPhee, and Puddle of Mudd.

Kara is also involved in a variety of charity works, and has raised money and built several recording studios at various locations of the nationally renowned youth outpatient substance abuse center Phoenix House. She also has a scholarship fund in her family's name, in conjunction with Columbus Citizens Foundation, which enables financially challenged Italian Americans the opportunity to attend college.